Note to Readers

While Fred and Alice's families are fictional, events in this book are based on historical fact. During the Great Depression, many families could no longer feed all their children. Parents had to ask their oldest children to leave home and provide for themselves. Thousands of teenagers became hobos who road on trains across the country, looking for work. Some of them were injured and killed trying to get on and off moving trains.

The Bonus Marchers, as they were called, actually marched into Washington, D.C., asking that they receive their promised bonus for fighting in the Great War. They wanted to get the bonus a few years early so that they could provide for their families. Against direct orders from President Hoover, General Douglas MacArthur ordered troops to attack the veterans. Some veterans were injured and killed.

And the Organized Unemployed company actually existed. A minister in Minneapolis came up with the idea as a way to help men who were without jobs provide for their families.

The
GREAT
DEPRESSION

JoAnn A. Grote

BARBOUR
PUBLISHING, INC.
Uhrichsville, Ohio

To Bruce and Becky Durost Fish, editors:
I enjoyed sharing the "Adventure" of working on the
American Adventure series with you.

ISBN 1-57748-475-4

Published by Barbour Publishing, Inc., P.O. Box 719, Uhrichsville, Ohio 44683
http://www.barbourbooks.com

 Member of the
Evangelical Christian
Publishers Association

Printed in the United States of America.

Cover illustration by Peter Pagano.
Inside illustrations by Adam Wallenta.

CHAPTER 1
The Lost Penny

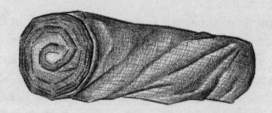

"Oh, no! It's gone!"

Alice Harrington looked in surprise at her red-headed friend Dot Lane. Dot was staring at the pennies in her hand. "What's gone, Dot?"

"One of my pennies. Mother gave me nine, just enough for the loaf of bread, and now there are only eight!"

The tears glistening in Dot's green eyes upset Alice. "Maybe you counted wrong. Let me try."

Dot slid the pennies into one of Alice's hands. Alice's short, curly blond hair slipped against her cheek as she counted the copper coins herself. Then she looked back at Dot. "Eight," she agreed. "Try your pockets again. The other penny must be there."

Alice watched Dot slip her hands into the pockets of her

faded green-and-white-checked gingham dress. "Oh, no! There's a hole in one pocket corner. The penny must have fallen out of the hole on our way."

"Maybe it fell out here in the store," Alice said. "Let's check the floor."

The two girls walked slowly toward the door on the other side of the room. They studied the wooden floor carefully. They knew it would be easy for an old penny to blend in with the dark wood or fall through the cracks of the wooden planks or slip beneath one of the many wooden bushel baskets that covered the floor.

The smells of the fresh fruits and vegetables in the baskets made Alice hungry. Each basket overflowed with something different: green beans, cucumbers, potatoes, celery, lettuce, onions, sweet potatoes, apples, peaches, wild plums. She ignored her growling stomach and kept looking for the penny.

Alice scrunched her face into a scowl. She waved a hand in front of her face, trying to chase away a pesty, noisy fly. Sticky yellow strips hung from the ceiling to trap the flies that liked the fruits and vegetables, but the strips hadn't trapped this one yet. The strips swung in the breeze made by the large ceiling fan that kept warm July air moving.

The girls had almost reached the front of the store when a tall, skinny young man with a white jacket over his shirt and tie asked, "Are you girls looking for something? Can I help you?"

Alice knew he was a clerk in the store. She'd seen him putting groceries into a wooden box, filling a grocery order for a customer. Hope made her smile. *Maybe he found Dot's penny while he worked,* she thought. "My friend lost a penny. Did you find one?"

He shook his head. "Sorry. Maybe one of the other clerks found it."

Alice glanced at the three men in white jackets who stood behind the tall wooden counter at the back of the store. All three were holding a telephone receiver to their ear with one hand; with the other hand they were making notes in pencil on tablets.

"I don't think so," she told the helpful man. "Those clerks have all been on the telephone taking orders for groceries since we came into the store."

"Too bad. Hope you find it." The man smiled and went back to work.

"We *must* find it," Dot told Alice. "When Mother gave me the pennies, she said they were all the money she had. And it takes nine pennies to buy a loaf of bread."

All the money she had? Alice tried to hide her horror at Dot's words. "If we don't find the penny, maybe your mother can bake some bread."

Dot shook her head. "We don't have enough flour or sugar left. It's cheaper to buy the loaf of bread than to buy the flour and sugar."

Alice saw unhappily that there were tears in Dot's eyes again.

Together they explored the rest of the floor all the way to the door. Alice knelt down so she could check whether the penny had rolled beneath the barrel of pickled cucumbers. "Nothing there," she said when she stood up. "I guess we better walk back to your house. Maybe we'll find it yet."

They went through the screen door that let fresh air into the one-room store and stepped out on the sidewalk.

Alice couldn't keep her gaze on the sidewalk looking for Dot's penny all the time. There were other brick stores and business buildings along this street. The street wasn't busy with cheerful shoppers the way it had been a couple years ago, when she and Dot had been ten years old. The depression had changed everything.

Many of the stores were empty now. Their windows were empty. The buildings looked dark and unfriendly. Even the buildings of stores and businesses that hadn't closed weren't very busy. There weren't many people who were shopping. In some of the windows, signs read, "No Help Needed." *I guess the owners of those stores are tired of men without jobs asking for work,* Alice thought.

They turned a corner and soon came on a bread line. The men were waiting for some bread and maybe soup at a mission. It was a long line, for the mission was two blocks away.

Most of the men who were on the sidewalks were leaning against walls or sitting on the curb. Some of them talked to each other, but most of them just watched the world go by with sad eyes in narrow faces. Some had a bedroll wrapped in canvas setting beside them. Some had dirty flour sacks. Alice's mother had told her these homeless, unemployed men probably carried everything they owned in those sacks. Alice felt sorry for them. Some of the men didn't even have flour sacks.

"If I lost the penny near here," Dot whispered to her, "one of these men probably found it and kept it."

Alice nodded. No one would pass up a penny lying on the sidewalk.

Dot's shoulders slumped. "I don't think we're going to find it. Mother will be so upset."

"It wasn't your fault. She'll know that." Alice tried to make her feel better. "Maybe you should ask your father for the penny."

"He went to Washington."

Alice stopped and stared at her. "Washington! What is he doing there?"

"He wants to join the Bonus Marchers. The Bonus Marchers are men who fought in the Great World War. Back then, the government told them that part of their pay for fighting would be a bonus of one thousand dollars, but they wouldn't get the bonus until 1945. So many of the men who fought in the war are out of work that they want to ask the president and congress to give them the money now. Bonus Marchers from all over the country are going to Washington."

"I know." Alice nodded. "I heard my parents talk about them. My father fought in the war, too. He was wounded and sent to the hospital at Fort Snelling in St. Paul to heal. That's where he met my mother. She was a nurse there."

Dot smiled. Her green eyes, which had looked so sad just moments before, sparkled. "That sounds romantic."

Alice smiled back. "I think so, too. Anyway, I hope your father gets his bonus."

Dot's smile faded. "Me, too."

Alice tried to think of something to cheer her up again. "Just think, he'll see the Capitol and the Washington Monument. I wish I could see them."

Dot nodded, but she didn't smile again. "The Foshay Tower was built because Mr. Foshay liked the Washington Monument."

I forgot! Now I made her feel worse! Alice thought. The Foshay Tower was the highest building west of Chicago. When it opened in 1929, Dot's father had worked in it. He'd had a very important job and made lots of money. Then Mr. Foshay lost all his money, and many of his employees lost their jobs. Dot's father had been one of them. He hadn't found another job during the more than two years since then, not a real job. Sometimes he found work for a few days at odd jobs or even for only one day or a few hours.

Dot cleared her throat. "Father is afraid if he doesn't get the veterans' bonus that he won't be able to keep feeding everyone. I heard him tell Mother. They were in the kitchen, and I was in the living room. He didn't know I heard him. He told her that it was hard enough to feed everyone when it was only him and Mother and me."

Alice didn't know what to say. She felt sad for her friend but didn't know how to help her.

Dot's family had moved from their beautiful big house to a little old house two years ago. Now Dot's grandmother and Dot's widowed aunt and three small cousins were living with them. The house was crowded, but Dot told Alice often how much she liked having her little cousins in the house. Dot liked little kids, and they liked her.

Alice looked again at the line of men that went for blocks. The words of a popular song by Yip Harburg went through her head:

Once I built a tower, to the sun.
    Brick and rivet and lime,
Once I built a tower,
    Now it's done—
Brother, can you spare a dime?
    Buddy, can you spare a dime?

It's men like these who have gone to Washington, Alice thought. *Men who risked their lives to fight for the country and now don't have money to buy food for themselves or their families.*

The girls turned the corner and left the sad area where the men were waiting in the hot summer sun for a small meal.

"Hi, Alice! Hi, Dot!"

Alice was jolted out of her thoughts about Dot by her cousin Fred Allerton's voice. His smiling face and eyes beneath strawberry blond hair lifted her spirits.

"Hi!" she answered. "What are you doing here?"

"I'm on my way to the movies. What are you two doing?"

"We went to the grocery store for Dot's mother," Alice told him. Alice glanced at Dot. *Maybe I'd better not tell him about Dot's penny,* she thought. *It might embarrass her.*

Fred grinned. "It doesn't look like you bought anything. Or are you carrying the groceries in your pockets?"

Alice bit her bottom lip and didn't answer.

"I was carrying my money in my pocket," Dot told him, "but I have a hole in my pocket and lost some. When we got to the store, I didn't have enough money left."

"Boy, that's tough." Fred's blue eyes grew troubled. "How much did you lose?"

Alice watched Dot. This time it was Dot who bit her lip. Then Dot said, "A penny. All I was going to buy was a loaf of bread, but I can't buy it without that penny."

Alice was proud of Dot. She knew it hadn't been easy for Dot to tell Fred about the penny. When Dot's father had made a lot of money, Dot had been very proud and would have thought a penny was nothing to worry about.

"Dot's father is in Washington with the Bonus Marchers," Alice told Fred, "so she can't ask him for more money, and her mother doesn't have any more in the house."

Fred dug his hand into the pocket of his brown knickers and pulled out a dime. He held it out to Dot. "All I have is this dime for the movies, but you can borrow it if you'd like."

Dot's green eyes opened wide in surprise. "I. . .I couldn't take a whole dime from you. Especially if it's all you have."

"It's all right. I didn't mean it's all the money I have of my own. I meant it's all the money I have with me." He shrugged his shoulders, as if it didn't matter to him one way or another if he had any money, though Alice knew he was proud of his savings. "I have twelve dollars in an account at the bank."

"Twelve dollars!" Dot stared at him. "Where did you get so much money?"

"Father helped me open a savings account a long time ago. He wanted me to learn to save my money. Anyway, I don't mind lending you the dime." He held it out again.

Dot put her hands behind her back. "I can't."

Alice thought Dot looked at the dime like she really wanted to take it, even though she said she couldn't.

"Sure you can," Fred said. "Tell you what, if you don't want to borrow all of it, you can give me the money you have right now."

"Well, maybe that would work." Dot's eyes grew troubled. "Mother and Father don't believe in borrowing from people when he doesn't have a job. And if I borrow your dime, you won't have enough money to go to the movies."

Fred looked at the ground and kicked at a pebble. "Aw, that doesn't matter. It's just a movie. I can go another day."

"Thanks," Dot said quietly. "I have eight cents. If I used the dime to buy the bread, I'd get a penny in change. I could give that back to you and then I'd only owe you one penny."

"Sounds fair to me," Fred said.

Dot took the dime. Then she held out the fist in which she clutched the pennies and dropped the sweaty coins into Fred's hand. "I didn't dare put them back into my pocket," she told Alice. "The first thing I'm going to do when I get home is stitch up that hole!"

Alice smiled at her. "I guess we'd better go back to the store and buy that bread. Coming, Fred?"

"Sure."

As the three friends walked along, Alice's thoughts were troubled. She was glad her cousin had lent Dot the money for the bread, but Dot's family needed a lot more help than one penny or one dime.

They turned the corner where hundreds of men were still waiting in the bread line. Her heart felt sad. There were so many people who needed help. She and Fred sure couldn't help everyone, but she wished they could. She wished she had millions of dollars and could give everyone jobs. Then no one would have to stand in bread lines or be homeless.

But she didn't have millions, and she couldn't help everyone.

All I can do is stay friends with Dot, Alice thought.

CHAPTER 2
Caught!

Fred eagerly looked out the windows of his father's car. They were leaving the Gateway, where Nicollet and Hennepin Avenues met. The huge Hotel Nicollet stood right between the avenues, where they became one street almost three times as wide as a normal street.

Fred liked this part of the city. It was always bustling with people and cars.

The train depot, where they were headed, was only a short way ahead. The buildings they passed as they neared it weren't as grand as the Hotel Nicollet. Here there were employment agencies, and "flop houses"—cheap places for men to sleep. Racks of overcoats and men's pants stood in front of little stores. Fred knew the clothes were padlocked to the racks to keep people from stealing them.

14

Everywhere, men stood or sat, lounging about, looking dejected. *How many of them are homeless men?* Fred wondered. *How many of them have lost their jobs and their homes and their savings because of the depression?*

The questions made his chest hurt. There didn't seem to be any way to stop the depression the country was in. He wished he could help each of these men, but he knew that wasn't possible. The men who ran the country and states and cities and businesses would have to find a way to help them.

He was glad when they reached the depot and left the depressing scene behind them. The depot was built beside the Mississippi River, near St. Anthony Falls. The slightly fishy smell of the river mixed with the oil and soot and metal smells of the trains in a way that made Fred's heart beat a little faster.

His heart beat faster still when they entered the station with its large waiting room. It was crowded with people arriving and leaving and the people who were there to meet travelers or see them off. All the people made the already warm July evening even hotter.

Fred had to raise his voice to be heard above the sounds of the people and trains. "Do you see them?" he asked his father. He stretched his neck, trying to look over the crowd. He couldn't see any of the Harringtons or the Moes.

"Not yet." His father was looking over and around heads, too.

Someone yanked on Fred's sleeve. "Hi!"

He glanced down and grinned. "Hi, Alice. We were looking for your family."

She pointed across the room to where the gates opened into the train shed. "We're over there. So are Uncle Erik and Aunt Esther. We want to be where we can see Addy as soon as she comes into the station."

Fred and his parents followed her across the room, weaving through the crowd.

Aunt Esther's eyes were sparkling. She grabbed Fred's mother's hands. "She's coming home, Frances. Addy is coming home!"

Mother laughed. "I know, dear."

Fred and Alice grinned at each other. They all knew. It was why they were at the station house. Uncle Erik and Aunt Esther's daughter, Addy, was coming home from the sanatorium. She'd been there for three-and-a-half years. She had gone away when she was sixteen, hoping her tuberculosis would be cured at the sanatorium for tuberculosis patients.

It had been cured. Fred knew how blessed they were that Addy was cured. Two-thirds of TB patients died, even with the best treatments.

Fred glanced at the huge clock high on the wall. He leaned close to Alice so she could hear him. "It's fifteen minutes until Addy's train is due. Let's go outside for a bit. It's too hot in here."

Alice nodded.

Father agreed they could go out. "Be sure you are back by the time the train arrives. We don't want to lose you." He held up a finger in warning. "Mind you, don't get too close to the trains. They can be dangerous."

When they were back outside, Fred fanned his face with his hat. "Phew! It sure feels better out here. Let's go around the station house so we can see the trains coming."

The train house was between the station house and the river. It was very wide and long so that many trains could be inside at one time. The roof was curved like an upside-down bowl. Passengers could go into the train house from the station house. That way, they didn't get wet if it was raining or snowing.

"Should we watch the trains coming or going?" Alice asked.

"Coming," Fred decided.

"I wish I were coming or going," Alice said. "It would be fun to travel, wouldn't it?"

"Sure would."

They leaned up against a long, high cement wall that kept people away from the dangerous tracks. Looking over the top of it, they watched a train winding across the Mississippi toward them on the stone arch bridge James Hill had had built back in the 1800s. Fred could tell the train was slowing as it neared the depot on the tracks that ran along the river's edge. Still, its brakes squealed when it entered the yard.

Fred flinched at the sound, and Alice threw her hands over her ears.

Alice pointed toward the end of the train. "Why are those people getting off? Why don't they wait until the train stops in the train shed, so they don't get hurt?"

Fred's gaze followed hers. "Those are hobos. They didn't pay to ride the train. That's the same as stealing from the railroad. That's why they don't want to go into the station house. If they did, they'd be caught."

While they watched, people jumped down from the open door of a baggage car. There were men his father's age and men who were younger. There was even a family: a man with his wife and two little children.

As soon as the hobos were off the train, they hurried over the tracks.

"Where are they going?" Alice asked.

"Anywhere they can that will keep them from being seen until they can get out of the train yard and into the city."

"They are homeless people, aren't they?" Alice's voice was quiet.

Fred could tell she was upset. "Yes."

17

"I thought hobos were the men and boys who stop at the house. You know the ones I mean. The ones who ask if they can do some chores for us, and we give them something to eat."

Fred nodded. He knew. Almost every day someone like that stopped at their back door.

"I didn't know they rode trains like this, too," Alice said. One of the last hobos to leave the train was a tall, slender boy with a skinny face. The boy carried himself straight and tall, with his shoulders thrown back. *He looks proud,* Fred thought. He was wearing a hat like Fred's, the same kind of hat all the boys wore, so Fred couldn't see what color his hair was. Even though it was warm out, he wore a loose-fitting jacket over his dark shirt.

"He doesn't look much older than us," Alice said. "I sure wouldn't want to be riding across the country in a baggage car."

"Me, either."

There was a shrill whistle, then a shout. "Hey, there! Stop, all of you!"

Fred whirled to see who was calling. "Railroad detectives!"

Two men in uniforms that looked like policemen's uniforms were racing down the track toward the hobos. Each carried a club in one hand.

The hobos were scattering as fast as their legs would take them. They were heading down the tracks in the direction from which the train had come. Fred could see they had to get past the high wall before they could get out of the train yard.

From where they stood, Fred could see some of the hobos hiding behind other train cars. Some hid between cars that were hitched together.

Some of the hobos managed to get away, but not all of them. Fred held his breath while he watched one of the detectives chase after the tall, skinny boy. Would the boy get away? "Run!" he urged under his breath. He knew riding the railroad

18

without paying was wrong, but for some reason, he didn't want this boy caught.

The boy was running flat out, his coat flying behind him.

"Go!" Fred urged again.

"He's going to make it." Alice's voice was full of excitement. "He can run a lot faster than those old detectives."

Another train was coming over the bridge, heading toward the train yard. *What if the boy doesn't see it?* Fred wondered, his heart hammering. *What if he runs across the wrong track and gets hit?*

The boy tripped over a railroad tie. He sprawled face down in the gravel.

Fred groaned.

The boy jumped when the train's whistle blew. The brakes began squealing. With a sigh of relief, Fred saw the train wasn't on the same track as the boy.

Before the boy could even get to his knees, the detective was beside him.

The incoming train cut off Fred and Alice's view of the boy and the detective. Disappointed, Fred turned from the wall. "We'd better get inside. That might be Addy's train."

"I'd forgotten all about Addy!" Alice hurried along beside him. "And I'm so excited she's coming home!"

Once again, Fred and Alice wove their way through the crowd in the station house until they reached their families. They watched the gate eagerly, waiting for their first glimpse of Addy.

"Do you think we'll recognize her?" Alice asked.

Fred shrugged. "I don't know. Three-and-a-half years is a long time."

Alice giggled. "Maybe she won't recognize us."

Fred didn't answer. He was staring at the gate. Passengers

were standing aside while the railroad detectives directed the hobos from the train shed into the station house.

All about them, people stopped their conversations to point at the hobos and whisper. Fred saw one woman step back, holding the skirt of her dress back, too, as if she were afraid one of the hobos might brush against her and get her dress dirty. The hobos did look like they could use baths, Fred admitted, and their clothes were rumpled.

When the boy they'd seen earlier walked past, Fred's chest felt like it would explode. The boy's cheeks were red and dirty. *Is the dirt from when he fell?* Fred wondered. He was pretty sure the red cheeks were because the boy was embarrassed. The boy was looking straight ahead, ignoring the whispering people who watched him. His dark eyes looked stormy.

A minute later, the crowd closed in where the hobos had been, and train passengers began entering the station house.

"There's Addy!" Aunt Esther called out. She waved eagerly. "Addy! Over here, Addy!"

A tall girl with curly dark brown hair and a huge smile waved back. She had sparkling green eyes, like Aunt Esther's.

"I guess we didn't have to worry about recognizing her," Fred said to Alice. "She looks a lot like she did before she went away, only older."

Alice nodded. "And prettier." She was waving at Addy.

Soon Addy was surrounded by family. Uncle Erik and Aunt Esther were trying to hug her at the same time. Everyone was laughing because they were so happy to see her.

Something drew Fred's glance across the room. He could see the back of the boy and one of the detectives as they left the building. The happiness he felt at seeing Addy clouded over.

The boy had received quite a different welcome to Minneapolis than Addy had.

CHAPTER 3

A Surprise Encounter

"I didn't know people could eat dandelions!" Alice said to Dot the next week when the girls and Fred were in the park.

"Oh, yes." Dot pulled green dandelion leaves from the ground and dropped them into the basket beside her. "Sometimes Mother cooks them in bacon grease, and sometimes we have them for a salad. They're really very good."

Fred wrinkled his nose, making a face at Alice behind Dot's back. *I sure wouldn't want to try them,* he thought. He squatted down beside Dot and began helping her pick the dandelion leaves.

"We've learned to eat all kinds of things since Father lost his job," Dot said.

"They even turned their front lawn into a garden," Alice told Fred.

"We couldn't grow very much in our backyard." Dot giggled. "Father says it's no bigger than a postage stamp." Her face grew serious. "Last night, someone stole all the green beans."

"Stole them right out of your front yard?" Fred couldn't imagine someone being so bold.

Dot nodded. "Mother said from now on, she and I and Aunt Wilma will have to take turns staying up at night and watching the garden. We don't want to lose any more food."

Fred saw something small and round in the grass and reached for it.

"What's that?" Alice asked.

"I think it's a walnut," Fred answered, "but it's not ready to eat yet."

Dot jumped up and stared into the tree's branches. "A walnut tree! I'll have to remember that. In September, I can come back and collect nuts."

Dot isn't anything like the spoiled, selfish girl she was before her father lost his money, Fred thought. He rather admired her. "You sure have learned a lot about how to get food without paying money for it, Dot."

She shrugged, and her cheeks grew pink. "We had to learn. It used to embarrass me, but now so many people are out of work and poor like us, that I'm not embarrassed anymore." Her eyes sparkled. "Guess what Aunt Wilma and I did yesterday?"

"What?" Alice and Fred asked at the same time.

"We went fishing in the Mississippi River!"

"Did you catch anything?" Fred asked. He always liked fishing.

Dot nodded. "The fish were pretty wiggly. Aunt Wilma took them off the hook for me. The worst part was catching nightcrawlers." She shuddered and made a face.

Fred and Alice laughed. Fred couldn't imagine Dot out in the dark looking for nightcrawlers to use as bait.

"Oh, look at the rabbit!" Alice pointed to a brown rabbit that was chewing some grass nearby.

It wiggled its ears. Its eyes darted about. Then it took off toward a clump of bushes. After a few hops, it stopped to look around. Then it started off again. Suddenly in the middle of a hop, it fell, landing on its side.

The three friends jumped to their feet. "What happened?" Alice asked. "It's not moving!"

Fred started toward it, and the girls followed. Fred had only taken a couple steps when he saw a tall, skinny boy a few years older than himself loping toward the rabbit. The boy carried a slingshot in one of his hands. "So that's what happened," he said under his breath.

"Hey, that's my rabbit! Leave it alone!" the boy yelled as Fred stopped beside the still rabbit.

Fred could see in a flash the rabbit was dead. He hated to see it had been killed, but part of him had to admit the boy was a mighty good shot with a slingshot.

The boy reached them, bent over, and picked up the rabbit by its ears.

"You killed it!" Alice accused, her hands balled into fists at her sides. "You didn't have to kill it!"

The boy stared at her with dark eyes from beneath the visor of his hat. He didn't say anything.

The boy was wearing worn brown trousers and a corduroy jacket, with a shirt that used to be white. His clothes looked rumpled and a bit dusty.

Surprise rolled through Fred. *Why, it's the boy who was arrested at the railway station!*

23

"Why did you kill that rabbit?" Alice demanded.

Fred took hold of one of her arms. "I think it's his dinner," he said quietly.

The boy's chin went up with a proud air. "Yeah, it is. What's it to ya?"

Alice didn't answer. She only folded her arms and stared at the rabbit.

Fred hoped she understood that if the boy was killing a rabbit in the park for food, he probably didn't have money to buy food.

"We were just picking dandelion leaves for dinner," Fred told him. *Maybe if he thinks we're eating "free" food, too, he'll be friendlier,* he thought. "My name is Fred. This is my cousin Alice and our friend Dot."

The boy glanced at the basket of dandelion greens Dot was carrying. He seemed to relax just a little. "I'm Chet Strand."

Fred pointed at the slingshot that Chet was still holding. "You're really good with that. Can I see it?"

Chet held it out to him.

Fred pulled at the rubber sling, testing its strength. "Pretty tough. How did you make it? I mean, I can see the rubber bands, but what is this sling made from?"

"First, you have to find a strong piece of wood with a fork in it. Then you cut holes in the top of the fork, so you can tie rubber bands through them. You cut a piece from a worn-out tire for the middle of the sling. It holds the shot a lot better than a plain rubber band. Cut a hole in each side of the tire piece, too, and hook a rubber band through each side. Works swell."

"I can tell." Fred handed it back reluctantly. "You're a great shot."

Chet grinned at him. "Thanks."

"You're the hobo boy we saw arrested at the railroad station," Alice said quietly.

Chet's back stiffened.

Fred bit back a groan. Chet's grin was gone, and his face looked stiff. Fred was sorry Chet might not act friendly anymore, but he was more worried about what Alice might tell their parents. Both of them had strict orders to stay away from the parks and riverside areas where hobos tended to stay, but Fred had never noticed hobos in this park before.

"Are you really a hobo?" Dot's eyes were shining.

Chet glared at her.

Dot didn't seem to notice that he seemed angry at her question. She kept talking. "Because if you are, there're some things I'd like to ask you."

Chet kept glaring at her.

What does she want to ask him? Fred wondered. He couldn't figure out why Dot, of all people, would want to talk to a hobo.

Dot stamped her foot impatiently. "Well, are you a hobo or aren't you?"

"Yes."

"Oh, good!"

Chet looked at her as if she were nuts. Fred thought she was sounding pretty nuts, too.

"My father went to Washington with the Bonus Marchers," Dot explained. "Have you heard about them?"

Chet nodded. "Sure. The first bunch of them started out from Oregon. Then other veterans from all over the country heard they were going to Washington and joined them. They're living in abandoned government buildings and in shacks around Washington."

Dot nodded. "That's right. My father doesn't have a car or

25

money for a train or bus ticket, so he was going to try to ride the trains like the hobos."

"Oh, I see," Chet said. "Lots of men like your father are doing that these days."

"I've been really worried about him," Dot said. "We haven't heard from him since he left. Congress decided not to give the men their bonus. The news reports say the men are going to stay in Washington until Congress changes its mind, even if it takes years. But even so, I think Father will be coming home pretty soon. Is it awfully dangerous, riding on the trains like you do?"

Chet's face grew more friendly. "It's not so bad. A bit uncomfortable."

"What if he fell off and hurt himself?"

"That happens to fellows sometimes," Chet admitted, "but not to so many as you might think. Most hobos don't get hurt. Some of the hobos who have been around a while will give your father some tips, tell him how to get around the bulls, the safest ways to get on and off the trains. He'll be all right."

"Then the hobos won't hurt him?" Dot asked.

Fred thought he saw a flicker of anger cross Chet's face, and then it was gone.

"Hobos aren't bums," Chet told her. "Hobos are gentlemen down on their luck, that's all. There's a couple bad apples among them, like there is anywhere else, but mostly they're good men. Your father is probably as safe riding the rails as he is at home in his bed."

Dot grinned at him. "Thanks. I've really been worried about him."

Chet smiled at her.

"What are 'bulls'?" Fred asked.

"Railroad detectives," Chet told him. "Most every station has bulls these days because there're so many hobos riding the rails."

"Did they take you to jail when they caught you?" Alice asked Chet.

Chet shot her a dirty look. "Just overnight. Could have been worse. In some towns, the bulls aren't honest men. They steal any money the hobos have. I've been in towns where the bulls run along beside every train that leaves, looking on top of the trains and beneath them and between the cars and in the cars. They carry guns and clubs."

Dot's face grew pale. "I hope Father doesn't run into any bulls."

"If he doesn't have any money for them to take and he doesn't run away when they spot him, he'll be okay," Chet told her.

"What if they put him in jail like they did to you?" Dot asked.

Chet grinned. "He'll probably thank them. At least he'll have a bed to sleep in for one night."

"Do you always get put in jail if you're caught?" Fred asked. It was hard for him to imagine all this boy had seen and experienced. Their lives were so different.

"Naw. Sometimes the bulls make us work to pay for riding the train, doing things like fixing the railroad tracks or shoveling coal on the trains." Chet shrugged. "I don't mind. It's only fair to work in return for riding. I wouldn't mind doing it all the time, but if you ask for work to pay for the ride before you catch the train, they'll tell you there isn't any work to be done."

"Would you like to come have supper with us?" Fred asked.

Chet looked like he wanted to say yes, Fred thought, but he shook his head. "This rabbit will be good to put in the stew at the hobo jungle tonight. Lots of nights there isn't any meat for the stew. I'd hate to let the other hobos down."

Alice's eyebrows drew together. "What's a jungle?"

"That's where hobos stay," Chet explained. "There's always a stew cooking over the fire. Everyone who eats the stew has to bring something to put in it. The stew is more water than anything else, but we get by."

Alice still looked confused. "I thought jungles were called 'Hoovervilles,' after President Hoover."

"Yeah." Chet nodded. "Some guys call them that."

"Have. . .have you looked for a job in Minneapolis?" Fred asked him.

"Yes. Haven't had much luck. Not many jobs to be had, and most of the jobs there are go to men with families, not kids like me."

"How old are you?" Alice asked.

"Seventeen. Anyway, I think I'll catch a train out of Minneapolis soon. Harvest is starting. Maybe I can find some work on a farm."

"Good luck," Fred told him.

Chet walked away. When he got near the sidewalk at the edge of the park, he turned and waved at them.

Fred and the girls waved back.

"I wish he would have come to dinner," Fred said. "It would have been interesting to talk to him some more."

"Your parents wouldn't want you to bring home a hobo for dinner," Alice reminded him.

"They feed the hobos who come to our house and ask for work and food," he said.

Still, he thought she was right. Feeding someone who came to your door begging was different than going out and making friends with a hobo. He couldn't help wondering about Chet. He felt sorry for him, but in some ways, he thought his life must be awfully exciting. *More exciting than mine, anyway.*

CHAPTER 4

Attack on the Marchers

"You don't have to help," Alice told Dot as she hoed weeds from the garden in the Harringtons' backyard.

"I don't mind," Dot told her. "We can visit easier if we're working together."

Alice liked working outside with the smell of the vegetables and the earth. The hoes made soft scraping sounds while they worked.

Alice's ten-year-old brother, Steven, and seven-year-old sister, Isabel, were working in the next row. The garden was their responsibility. It was a lot of hard work planting it and taking care of it, but they were proud of the food they raised for their family.

The garden helped the family save money. Alice's father worked long hours in the summer, but in the winter, the company cut the employees' hours.

Usually Alice's mother kept the two youngest children inside when the others were working in the garden. Four-year-old Frank and twenty-one-month-old Audrey were always pulling up plants instead of weeds or putting rocks in their mouths or causing trouble some other way when they were in the garden.

"Excuse me, miss."

Alice looked up in surprise at the man standing at the edge of the garden. He was about her father's age, very skinny, with gray and brown hair. His dusty clothes looked too big for him. He held his hat in his hands.

"Yes, sir?"

"Are your mother and father at home?" he asked. "I'd like to speak with them."

Alice was sure he didn't know her parents. He was a hobo, one of the many who stopped at their house every week. "My mother is home. I'll get her for you."

Her mother came with her to the back door, where the man waited on the wooden porch. Alice slipped past her mother and headed back to the garden, but she could hear her mother and the man talking.

Mother smiled at the man. "Hello. I'm Mrs. Harrington. What can I do for you, Mr. . . . ?" She waited for him to tell her his name.

"Walters, ma'am." The man shifted the dirty hat in his hands. "I was wonderin' if you had any chores that might need doin'?"

"Why, yes, I do. There's some wood next to the shed that needs to be cut into stove lengths for my laundry stove."

"Thank you, ma'am." Mr. Walters put his hat on and headed back toward the shed. Alice thought he walked a little straighter than before.

Even though their family had to be more careful with their money these days, her parents never turned a man away who stopped and asked for work or food. "It's important for a person to feel they've earned the things they need, like food," her father always said. "That's why we always leave wood to be cut by the men who stop or give them another chore to do. Some people think hobos just want a free handout, but I believe most people would rather work for what they get."

Listening to the ax thunk against the wood as Mr. Walters split logs, Alice remembered what her father had said. She thought she understood what he meant. After all, the peas and beans and lettuce and other vegetables they grew tasted much better when she had worked so hard to grow them than if they'd bought them from the store.

When the man had chopped the wood and carried it down the basement to where the laundry stove was kept, Mother handed him a broom. "To brush off the sawdust," she told him, but the man and everyone else knew she thought he needed to brush dust and dirt from his clothes, too. Alice liked the way her mother always tried to keep from hurting the hobos' feelings.

Since Father was home for dinner, Mr. Walters was invited to share their supper. Alice knew that if Father hadn't been home, Mother would have let Mr. Walters eat outside on the back steps instead. When the meal was over, Mr. Walters left.

Dot helped Alice with the dishes. "We have to hurry with them," Alice told her, "so we don't miss *Amos 'n' Andy*."

Mother took Frank and Audrey out of the room so they wouldn't get in the girls' way.

31

"Whenever I see little kids like Frank and Audrey," Dot told Alice, "I think about the Lindberghs' baby. How could anyone hurt a baby like that?"

"I don't understand it, either," Alice said quietly. "It hurts inside whenever I think about it."

That March, Charles Lindbergh's baby, a boy who was named for his famous flying father, had been kidnapped from his crib. The kidnappers had demanded money, and the Lindberghs gave them fifty thousand dollars, but they didn't get the baby back. Two months later, the baby was found dead.

"Do you think they will ever find the people who kidnapped and murdered the little Lindbergh boy?" Dot asked.

"I hope so," Alice told her. "I feel so sorry for Colonel Lindbergh and his wife. If anything like that happened to Audrey or Frank, I'd feel awful."

"At least there are new laws against kidnapping now. Maybe that will help keep people from snitching babies."

The girls slipped into the living room and dropped onto the floor beside Alice's brothers and sisters just as the radio program started. Laughter filled the room until the show was over and the news began.

Dot stood up. "I'd better go home."

Just then, the news reporter began talking about the Bonus Marchers. "There's trouble in Washington tonight," said a deep voice. "As I speak, American troops and tanks are chasing Bonus Marchers—men who fought for us in the Great War—from our nation's capital."

Dot sank back to the floor. Alice glanced at her. Dot knelt, staring at the radio, her green eyes large.

Father turned up the radio.

Mother shushed the younger children. She picked up Audrey and cuddled her in her lap to keep her quiet.

"Earlier today," the reporter continued, "police were ordered to put Bonus Marchers out of the abandoned government building where they had been living. While the police were following orders, vets surged about them. A policeman has told us that veterans were throwing bricks at the police. The police opened fire on the veterans. Details of the event are not known yet, but at least two of the men are seriously injured and may be dead."

Dot gasped. She clasped her hands to her mouth.

CHAPTER 5

An Exciting Plan

Alice's heart leaped to her throat. *What if Dot's father is one of the men who was shot? What if he's dead?*

Mother reached out and rubbed one of Dot's shoulders.

The radio report went on. "At four-thirty this afternoon, General Douglas MacArthur led American troops from near the White House down Pennsylvania Avenue. First came the cavalry, then the army, then tanks. At first, the Bonus Marchers cheered the troops, saluting them as they passed. Their cheers turned to cries of fear as the cavalry began pushing the veterans back with the flat sides of their swords. After they'd pushed the veterans many blocks back, the soldiers put on gas masks and carried bayonets. They tossed tear gas bombs into abandoned buildings where Bonus Marchers were staying, forcing the veterans out of the buildings."

Tears ran down Dot's face. Alice's chest hurt because she felt so sorry for her friend.

"Right now," the reporter's deep voice said, "orange flames are shooting up from the main camp of the Bonus Marchers. Hundreds of tents and lean-tos built of newspapers, cardboard boxes, and packing crates are being burned by the army. The Bonus Marchers and any wives and children with them have been cleared out. Smoke and the smell of burning cloth fill the air. Ambulances are carrying off men who have been injured. Many men's eyes are still streaming from the tear gas."

Dot's sobs broke into the room. Alice put an arm around her shoulder, wishing she could make her friend feel better.

The reporter switched to other news, and Father turned off the radio.

"How could they do that?" Mother asked Father, her voice filled with horror. "How could our army attack those people?"

Father's face looked grim beneath his dark curly hair. "I don't understand. When the Senate voted against giving the men the bonus, the men didn't cause any trouble. The men filled the Capitol steps, waiting for the news. When it came, all they did was sing 'America.' "

"The Bonus Marchers love this country," Mother said. "They fought for it."

Father nodded. Alice thought he looked very tired. "This is a sad day for our country," he said.

Dot's sniffs and sobs broke into their conversation. She dashed away tears with the back of her hand.

"Find Dot a clean handkerchief, Alice. Then I think Father

and I should walk Dot home. It's getting dark. Does that sound all right to you, Dot?"

Dot nodded.

"If your mother hasn't heard the news yet," Mother told Dot, "Mr. Harrington and I can help you tell her. Alice, you and Steven put the other children to bed while we're gone."

"Yes, Mother." Alice hurried out of the room to get the handkerchief. *What if Dot's father is hurt, or. . .or dead?* she wondered, hurrying up the steps to her bedroom. "Please, God, don't let him be hurt," she whispered.

At church Sunday, Alice and her family slid into the pew beside Dot and her mother. Fred's family sat in the pew in front of them, as usual. Fred whispered something to his mother then moved back to sit beside Alice, smiling at her as he sat down.

"Have you heard from your father?" Alice whispered to Dot.

Dot shook her head no. Alice was sorry she'd asked when she saw Dot's eyes grow red and glisten with unshed tears.

When Pastor Mecklenburg got up to give the sermon, Alice was surprised. It wasn't like any sermon she'd heard before. He faced the congregation, leaning on the podium with straight arms. "I cannot see people hungry and go on preaching," he said.

Alice stared at him. So did everyone else. The sanctuary became very still. *Is he going to stop being our pastor?* Alice wondered. She leaned forward, eager to hear what he said next.

"I cannot keep preaching," he started again, "unless I do something to help the people in our city who are jobless and hungry. And that is what I intend to do; help them."

Alice breathed a sigh of relief. *How is he going to help them?*

"I'm going to help them to help themselves," Pastor Mecklenburg said. "We hear a lot of people complaining that President Hoover and Congress and the Minnesota governor should be giving unemployed people free food or money they don't need to pay back." He held up his hands. "I'm not talking about the Bonus Marchers. Those men earned their bonus by fighting in the war."

Alice smiled at Dot, and Dot smiled back.

"I believe most of the men without jobs do not want to be given food or clothing or money or anything else they haven't earned," the pastor said. "I believe they are only asking the government to help them this way because they don't know what else to do. They've tried getting jobs. Many homeless and unemployed men look for jobs every day."

Like Dot's father, Alice thought.

"I believe," Pastor Mecklenburg continued, "that men want to work, that having a job makes a man feel good about himself. He'd rather eat food he earned himself than eat food someone gave him out of pity."

Alice saw men in the congregation nodding. They agreed with the pastor. Alice sat up straighter. *Why, that's the way I feel about the food we grow in the garden! It tastes better because we worked so hard to grow it ourselves. Is that the way men feel about their work, too?*

Fred whispered in her ear, "That's what Chet said, that hobos aren't bums. They want to work for what they get."

Pastor Mecklenburg rubbed his hands together and smiled. "I've prayed about the hungry men on our streets, and this is what I think we should do. I'm going to start a company called Organized Unemployed. And that's just what we're going to do. We're going to help the unemployed men get organized into a company."

Alice and Fred looked at each other. "How can men without jobs form a company?" she asked him in a whisper.

He shrugged and shook his head.

Pastor Mecklenburg leaned forward. "I'm going to need your help to get this company going. Please donate anything you can. We'll need money, of course. But we'll also need ideas for work the men and women can do and the tools and supplies to do the work."

He straightened up, smiling. "Now, you may be wondering how we can pay the people who work in this company. I'll tell you. We are not going to pay them in money." He stopped talking and, still smiling, watched the congregation.

Alice glanced at Dot then at Fred. They both looked as surprised as she felt.

"We're going to use scrip," the pastor said. "For every hour a person works, they will be given scrip, a piece of paper worth twenty-five cents. Now, not every business in the city will let people pay with pieces of paper! That's another area where you men in the congregation can help. You can agree to let people buy things in your business with scrip."

Adults in the congregation began to shift in their seats. Some men shook their heads. *Do they think it's a silly idea?* Alice wondered. She had to admit, it sounded strange.

"One of the things we're going to do in the company is start our own store to sell what we make. Of course, people can buy the things from the company store with money, but they will also be able to buy them with scrip." Pastor Mecklenburg beamed at the congregation as if he didn't notice the men who were shaking their heads. "Let me know any way in which you can help our new company."

After the service, when everyone was slowly leaving the church, Alice listened to the adults talking about the Organized Unemployed company.

"Sounds like a dumb plan to me," one man said to another.

"Me, too," the man he was speaking to agreed. "I wouldn't

want anyone buying things from my store with pieces of worthless paper."

"I think it's worth a try," Alice's father told them.

"So do I," Fred's father said. "Not much else is working. Why not try something new?"

Alice and Fred smiled at each other. Warmth filled Alice's chest. She was proud of her father for sticking up for Pastor Mecklenburg's idea.

The men who disagreed didn't argue. They just changed the subject. "What about the army running out the Bonus Marchers?" one of them said.

"I fought in the Great War," the other told him. "I think it's shameful, the president letting the army do something like that."

All around them, people were nodding their heads.

"I fought in the Great War, too," Alice's father said. "It's a sad thing when the army of the most powerful nation on earth attacks its own unarmed citizens."

An old man with white hair and a white beard leaned forward. "I fought in the Spanish-American War back in 1898. Why, when I heard our soldiers had been ordered to attack their own people, I almost broke down and cried. I won't be votin' for Hoover again, no siree."

The men and women standing around all agreed with him.

When they reached the door where the pastor was shaking hands with everyone, Alice heard Fred's father say to the pastor, "I think your plan is a good one. I'll be glad to take scrip from my patients in return for services. And I know a man who would be a great help to you in getting the Organized Unemployed started."

"Who is that?" Pastor Mecklenburg asked.

"He's a man who used to work with Mr. Foshay, who built the Foshay Tower. He has a lot of good business experience.

He's just out of work now because of the depression. He's in Washington with the Bonus Marchers now, but when he gets back, I'll ask him to get in touch with you, if you'd like. His name is Mr. Lane."

Mr. Lane! Alice stared at her uncle. "That's Dot's father," she whispered to Fred.

Fred nodded, his blue eyes sparkling. "It's a great idea, isn't it?"

Pastor Mecklenburg seemed to think so, too. "Sounds like a good man," he told Uncle Richard. "Send him over!"

CHAPTER 6
A Surprise Visitor

A few days later, Dot hurried into the Harringtons' backyard, where Fred and Alice were talking. "Guess what!" A huge smile filled Dot's face.

"What?" Alice and Fred asked at the same time.

"Father is home from Washington!"

"Was he hurt by the army or police?" Alice asked.

Dot shook her head, still smiling. "No. Well, he did get a little scratch, but he said that happened when he fell down. He fell because all the Bonus Marchers were running, and there were so many of them. But no one hit him or anything."

"What else did he tell you about it?" Fred asked eagerly. "Was it as bad as it sounded on the radio?"

"Oh, it was awful!" Dot told him. "But I'll tell you about it another time. Right now, I have something else to tell you. Something wonderful has happened! Pastor Mecklenburg asked Father to help him with the new company, Organized Unemployed!"

Alice grinned at her friend. "That's great!" She felt like her whole heart was smiling. She hadn't seen Dot this happy in a long, long time.

"Your father will be good at that job," Fred said, "with all his business experience."

Dot beamed. Alice could see she was proud to hear Fred say such nice things about her father.

"He won't get paid at first," Dot told them, "not while he's helping to get it started. But later he'll get paid scrip, like everyone else."

"I think it's wonderful," Alice said in a quiet voice.

Two months later, on a Saturday in October, Alice hurried over to Dot's house. Colorful, dry leaves crunched under her feet as she went up the walk.

Dot opened the door. "Hi! What are you doing here?"

She doesn't look very glad to see me, Alice thought. "It's Audrey's birthday today, so Mother decided to have a party. She said I could invite you."

Dot frowned. "A party? Audrey's only turning two today. Isn't that young for a party?"

Alice shrugged and pulled her cardigan tighter about her. "It's not like a real birthday party, with games and things. You don't have to bring a present. It's really only supper with birthday cake and ice cream for dessert. Fred's family will be there and Addy's family. Mother says she's tired of the long faces everyone has because of the depression. She thought maybe the dinner and birthday cake would cheer people up. Can you come?"

"I'll ask my mother."

Dot turned to go back inside. Alice started to open the storm door to go inside and wait for Dot. Dot swung around and grabbed the door handle. "Wait here. I'll be right back." She pulled the storm door shut then shut the door to the house.

Alice stared at the closed doors in surprise, shivering in the fall wind. *Why is she acting so mean? She's always let me in her house before!* Then Alice remembered that she hadn't been to Dot's house for a couple months. Maybe Dot was upset she hadn't come over more often.

A minute later, Dot was back with her worn coat over her arm. "Mother says I can go." She was smiling as if nothing had happened.

Maybe she wasn't mean to me on purpose, Alice thought as they went down the sidewalk together. She tried to forget the incident as she listened to her friend talk about the walnuts she'd collected at the park and laid out to dry.

While Fred and Addy's mothers helped Alice's mother get the dinner ready, Alice and Dot talked with Addy in the living room.

"Are you really over your TB now?" Dot asked Addy.

Addy's brown curls bounced as she nodded her head. "I sure am!"

"I wonder how our friend Inez's mother is doing," Dot said.

"Do I know Inez?" Addy asked.

"She was a friend of ours from school," Alice told her. "Her mother has TB and was sent to a sanatorium. But Inez's family moved away, and we don't know where they are living now."

"A lot of people have moved the last couple years," Addy

said quietly. "With the depression, many people can't afford their homes anymore."

"That's why my aunt and grandma live with us," Dot said.

"Do you still want to be a nurse?" Alice asked Addy. "You wrote me from the sanatorium that you thought you wanted to be one."

Addy's face brightened. "Oh, yes. I'd like best to be a nurse to TB patients at a sanatorium. I need to go to school to be a nurse, though. I can't afford it right now."

"That's too bad," Dot said.

Addy smiled. "I don't mind waiting. At least, not too much. I'm volunteering at one of the local hospitals now as a nurse's aide, so I'm learning while I wait. I'm looking for a job, too, so I can make money to pay for school. But it's hard to find work, as you know."

Isabel came running into the room and threw herself against Addy's legs. "Won't you come upstairs with me, Addy? I want to show you something."

"Sure, I'll come."

When Addy and Isabel went upstairs, Alice and Dot wandered to the backyard. There the boys were playing with their hoops and sticks. The men were sitting on the back-porch steps, watching the boys and visiting.

Alice's father was shaking his head back and forth. "I won't vote for Hoover, that's for sure. Not after the way he treated our veterans."

Alice groaned and rolled her eyes at Dot. Next month was the election for president of the United States. It seemed to her the adults were talking about it all the time. She was tired of hearing about it!

The man running against President Hoover was Franklin D. Roosevelt. He'd traveled around the country on a train called the Roosevelt Special, trying to talk people into voting for him. Alice had seen lots of posters in store windows saying, "Abolish Bread Lines; Vote for Roosevelt."

"I agree with Donald," Uncle Erik, Addy's father, said. "Besides, Hoover sure hasn't done anything to help the men who are without jobs."

"Because he hasn't given out handouts?" Fred's father asked them. "Hoover's tried to make the money situation better. He got together the wealthiest, most powerful men in business and banking and asked for their advice and help. He doesn't even take his $75,000-a-year salary."

"What he's tried hasn't helped the country," Uncle Erik responded.

Fred's father sighed. "You're right, it hasn't. Things just keep getting worse. Roosevelt says he'll make things better, but he doesn't tell us how. I'm not sure Roosevelt will make a better president than Hoover, but with fifteen million men out of work, the country needs a change. Come election day, I'll be voting for Roosevelt alongside you two."

Alice squeezed past the men and hurried toward the garage, tired of listening to politics. Dot followed close behind.

At the garage, Fred and Steven were playing with their hoops. Some of the neighbor boys were playing, too. The hoops were old wheels with the spokes removed. Most of the hoops were from old baby carriages the boys had found at the dump. The best ones had rubber tires.

Hollers and pounding shoes on the dirt alleyway filled the air as the girls neared the alley.

Alice didn't have a hoop of her own, but sometimes Steven or Fred let her play with theirs. Today the boys were racing their hoops past the garage, using their curved sticks to guide the hoops. Steven was standing behind the garage, because he was "it." When the others rolled their hoops past the garage Steven would try to guess when they were near him. Then he'd roll out his hoop and try to hit one of the other boys' hoops. If he hit one, that boy would become "it." Sometimes the boys played the game for hours.

"It would be fun to have our own hoops, wouldn't it?" Dot asked as they watched the boys.

"Yes, but I wouldn't want to go through the piles at the dump to find them," Alice told her.

"Hello. Do you live here?"

Alice swung around at the sound of the boy's voice. A tall, skinny boy in dusty clothes stood there. Alice's mouth dropped open. It was Chet Strand, the hobo boy!

CHAPTER 7
Troubles on the Farm

"Chet Strand! What are you doing here?" Fred was running toward them from the alleyway, holding his hoop in one hand and his stick in the other.

Chet pointed at the hoop. "I used to have one of those. Played with it all the time. Whenever Dad got tired of having me hanging around him, he'd say, 'Oh, go roll a hoop.' "

Fred and Alice laughed. Their fathers said that to them, too. Steven and the other boys were gathering about Chet, curious about the newcomer. Fred wished they'd go away. They might embarrass Chet.

"I didn't know you lived here," Chet said, glancing about uncomfortably.

"It's my house," Alice said.

"Do you think I could talk to your dad?" Chet asked.

"Sure." Alice pointed toward the men on the back porch. "He's the one with the curly brown hair."

"Thanks." Chet pulled off his hat. Fred could see that his brown hair needed a haircut.

"Who's that?" Steven asked.

"His name's Chet Strand," Fred told him.

"Is he a friend of yours?"

"Kind of." He didn't want to tell Steven that Chet was a hobo. Steven was a good kid and kind of quiet, but there was no telling what he might say if he knew the truth about Chet.

Fred couldn't hear what Chet and Uncle Donald were saying, but he could guess. Chet probably wanted to do some chores in return for a meal, like the other hobos who stopped at their houses.

Sure enough, he saw Uncle Donald point toward the wood pile, and Chet headed that way.

The back screen door opened. Aunt Lydia carried out a jar of cream and set it down beside Uncle Donald, saying something to him that Fred couldn't hear.

Uncle Donald looked up. "Alice, Dot!" He waved them near with one arm. "Come over and help us make the ice cream!"

As the girls dashed for the porch, Fred went over to the shed to talk with Chet.

Chet pushed his hat back on. He pulled off his jacket and laid it over the clothesline. With a grunt, he pulled the ax out of the stump where it was buried. "Watch out that I don't hit you with any chips," he warned Fred.

Fred backed off a short ways and watched as Chet swung. A few minutes later, Steven came over. Fred was surprised his friends had left, then thought they had probably gone home for supper.

48

"You're pretty good with your hoop and stick," Chet told Steven between swings. "You steer yours really well."

"Thanks." Steven pushed his straight, dark hair out of his eyes. "I like playing with it, but I'd rather have a scooter. All the fellows have them but me."

"Why don't you make one?" Chet asked.

"I wouldn't know how."

Chet rested the head of the ax on a log and wiped his forehead with the back of his hand. "I know how. It's easy. If you have an old pair of roller skates around that no one is using anymore, I'll show you how to use them to make the scooter."

Steven's face brightened. "I'll see if I can find some." He raced off toward the house, leaving his hoop and stick behind.

Chet began chopping wood again. Fred turned a thick log on end and sat down on it. He liked the smell of fresh wood that came from newly cut logs. "Did you find any harvest work?" he asked Chet.

Chet nodded. "Worked on a lot of different farms."

"Does it pay very well?" Fred grinned. "If it does, maybe I'll suggest it to my brothers, Harry and Larry. They could both use a good-paying job."

"Depends on the crop and the farmer. Farmers are short of cash now, like everyone else. One farmer I worked for let me sleep in the barn, gave me three meals a day, but only fifteen cents for each day's work."

Fred raised his eyebrows. "Fifteen cents for a whole day's work?"

"Yep. That wasn't as bad as it sounds, though. Lots of men are making less than that these days. One farmer I worked for was really hard up. I worked all day in his field. Come dusk, he gave me two ears of corn for the day's work."

"Wow! I thought farmers had it easy. They don't have to

49

worry about getting a paycheck. They can grow everything they need for food."

"I found out it's costing them more to grow the food than they can get for the food when they sell it. Then they can't pay the bank for their loans or for gas for their tractors and trucks."

"I never thought of that," Fred said slowly.

"One farmer I worked for had all his chickens stolen. His family went to church, and when he came home, they were gone. He told me some of his farmer neighbors started staying home from church because people without jobs from town would come out while they were gone and take things. So farmers don't always have it so easy."

"Boy, I guess not!"

Chet stopped chopping to wipe his forehead again. "Worst thing for me is the Farmers' Holiday that's going on right now."

Fred knew what he was talking about. Lots of farmers had started an organization called the Farmers' Holiday Association the previous spring. They worked together like a union to make things better for farmers.

In September, the Minnesota group had started a strike. They blocked highways to keep other farmers from bringing their milk and meat and vegetables to market. They wanted to keep food from being sold until people would pay more money for it. When one Minnesota farmer tried to get his truck through the striking farmers, he'd shot and killed one of the striking farmers.

People were angry about the Farmers' Holiday strike because there wasn't as much food at the grocery stores and meat markets. What food there was cost more than it did before the strike. But Governor Olson said farmers had a right to strike like any other workers.

Chet leaned the ax against the shed, picked up a saw, and began sawing the wood into stove-size chunks. "Can't blame the farmers for wanting higher prices, what with a quart of milk selling for only five cents and a farmer only getting two cents a pound for his hogs and two cents for a dozen eggs."

"It does sound bad," Fred agreed, "but even at those prices, lots of people can't buy food."

Chet stopped sawing to grin at him. "Don't I know it." The grind of the saw began again.

Fred felt his face grow hot. He'd forgotten for a moment that Chet was homeless and didn't have a job. *He just seems like a regular guy when we talk.*

"I have to say, though," Chet added, "when I saw farmers dumping their milk on the highway, it made me sick to my stomach. All the hungry men I've seen riding the rails and standing in lines for hours for a cup of soup and a piece of bread, and the farmers throw away good food!" He shook his head. "I understand they need better prices to make a living. Still, it was a hard thing to see."

Steven came running up to them, panting, a steel skate in each hand. "I found them! There's something wrong with one of them, so Mother said we can use them for the scooter."

Chet grinned at him. "Great. Doesn't matter if one of the skates is broken, because we only need one for the scooter."

Steven's father was crossing the lawn on his long legs, his hands in his trouser pockets. Fred was glad to see his dark eyes were friendly when he spoke to Chet. "My son Steven tells me you offered to show him how to make a scooter."

It seemed to Fred that Chet looked a little wary, as if he wasn't certain Uncle Donald was really friendly. *I suppose a lot of people treat him mean because he's a hobo,* Fred thought. A pang of sadness tightened his chest.

"Yes, sir," Chet answered Uncle Donald. "That is, if it's all right with you."

"It's fine with me." Uncle Donald laughed. "Steven's been pestering me for a scooter of his own all summer. What will you need besides the skates to make it?"

Chet told him what size pieces of lumber he'd need and what nails. "Scrap lumber will do."

Uncle Donald nodded and laid a hand on Steven's shoulder. "Why don't you stop at one of the lumberyards Monday after school and ask if they have any pieces like that? They usually have some scrap around they'll let a boy have for free."

"All right." Steven's eyes were shining. "When can you make it, Chet?"

Uncle Donald said, "If you don't have other plans late Monday afternoon, how about stopping back then?"

Chet squared his shoulders and nodded. "Sounds fine to me."

Fred thought Chet looked pleased that Uncle Donald had treated him as he would anyone else, as if his time was important and he might have more to do than stand around feeling sorry for himself.

"I'm Donald Harrington," Fred's uncle said, holding out his hand to Chet. "I'm afraid these boys have forgotten to introduce us."

Chet swiped his sweaty palm across his trousers and shook Uncle Donald's hand. "Chet Strand."

"Nice to meet you, Chet. Why don't you carry a load of this wood down the basement to the laundry stove. Then Steven can show you where to wash up. We'd be glad to have you join us for dinner tonight." Uncle Donald grinned. "It's our youngest daughter's second birthday. There's going to be cake and ice cream for dessert."

A wide grin crossed Chet's skinny face. "Thank you, sir. That sounds great!"

A warm feeling filled Fred's chest. He liked Chet, and he

liked the way Uncle Donald treated him. "If you don't mind," he told Chet, "I'd like to see how you make the scooter."

Chet shrugged. "I'll be glad to show you." He leaned down and picked up a piece of wood about ten inches long and a couple inches wide from the sawdust and log chips on the ground. "Do you think it's okay if I take this with me?"

"Sure."

Chet picked up some of the stove lengths he'd just cut. "Okay, pal," he said to Steven. "Lead the way to the basement."

CHAPTER 8
Chet's Story

Monday afternoon, Chet was true to his word and showed up at the Harringtons' house. He was sitting on the back porch talking to Alice and Isabel when Fred and Steven arrived.

"Hi, Chet! We got the lumber." Steven held up two pieces. Each was a couple feet long and two inches by four inches.

Chet studied the pieces. "They look just the right size."

Steven grinned.

"Hope you haven't been waiting long," Fred said to Chet. "I went with Steven to the lumberyard. The man there said we could have the scrap lumber, but we'd have to work for it. We both had to pick up bent nails for half an hour." He made a face. "I didn't mind working to pay for the stuff, but we knew you'd be waiting."

"That's all right. Why don't you get your skates, Steven, and we'll get started."

An hour later, it was almost done. Chet had taken one of the skates apart. He'd attached one set of wheels to one end of a two-by-four and the other set of wheels to the other end. Then he'd nailed the other two-by-four to the front of the piece with the skate. Finally, he pulled a piece of wood about eight inches long from his back pocket. "This is the last piece, the handle."

Fred took it from him. "It's smooth. Is this the piece you took with you Saturday?"

Chet nodded. "I smoothed it down so Steven won't get slivers from it."

"Thanks!" Steven grinned at him.

"You're welcome." Chet nailed it onto the top of the piece of wood that stood straight up. Then, with one hand on the handle, he grinned at Steven. "One scooter, all set for travel."

Steven whooped with joy and grabbed the handles. "I'm going to try it out." He headed toward the alleyway, stopped, and turned around. "Think I'll try it on the sidewalk first." He pushed it through the grass toward the front of the house. Before he made it out to the sidewalk, Aunt Lydia came to the back door and called them all in for supper.

When they went inside, Chet pulled a small wooden object from his pocket and held it out to Aunt Lydia. "Would it be all right if I gave this to Audrey for her birthday? I know it's a couple days late, but. . ." He shrugged.

Aunt Lydia took it from him. Fred leaned close to see what it was. "Why, it's a little bird carved from wood!" Aunt Lydia's eyes sparkled in delight. "It's lovely, Chet. Thank you. I'm sure Audrey will enjoy playing with it."

Fred took it from Aunt Lydia's hand and studied it. "Did you carve this?"

Chet's cheeks grew red. "Yeah. I like to whittle. It fills up the time when I'm riding the rails or. . .or waiting for something."

Like standing in a bread or soup line? Fred wondered.

"You're good at carving," Aunt Lydia said.

Chet smiled but looked a little embarrassed.

After dinner, Steven insisted everyone come outside and watch him try out his new scooter. "It works swell!" he told Chet breathlessly when he returned from a scoot down to the end of the block and back. A moment later, he was gone again, with seven-year-old Isabel and four-year-old Frank chasing after him.

Aunt Lydia drew Chet aside. Though she spoke softly, Fred could hear what she said. "If you'd like, I could wash your clothes for you. I'd like to do something special for you for making the scooter for Steven and the bird for Audrey. You could borrow a shirt and trousers from my husband while I wash your things. Of course, they'd be large for you, but you'd only have to wear them for a day."

"I. . .I'd like that, ma'am," Chet said in a low voice. "It's hard to keep clothes clean when. . .well, you know."

He means when you don't have a home, Fred thought. His chest clenched again in pain for his new friend.

"If you'll come back first thing in the morning," Aunt Lydia said, "I'll do your things with our laundry tomorrow."

Aunt Lydia and Uncle Donald went back inside, taking Audrey with them. Fred and Alice stayed outside with Chet. They sat down on the front steps together in front of the screened porch. Fred watched Steven turn the corner, Frank and Isabel still racing after him. "Guess he's going to go around the block."

"I like all your brothers and sisters, Alice," Chet said quietly. "They remind me of my own brothers and sisters."

Fred stared at him in surprise. It was the first time Chet had talked about his own family. "I never thought of you as having brothers and sisters," he said. "I guess I just thought. . .I don't know. . .that you didn't have a family."

"I have a family." Chet didn't look at him while he talked. He leaned his elbows on the stairs behind him and watched the street. "I come from a big family, like Alice does. I haven't heard anything from my family since I left home. I think about them a lot. I worry about my brothers and sisters. I'm the oldest, see. I used to help Mom out with them a lot—help them with their school work and stuff like that. You know, teach them the stuff older brothers and sisters always have to teach."

Fred and Alice nodded. A lump filled Fred's throat. It hurt. He wondered if Alice had a lump in her throat, too.

"It's October," Chet said. "They should be back in school. I wonder if they are. I worry about them, whether they'll be able to finish school. I don't want any of them to have to quit and go out on their own the way I've had to do. I'd like to get a good-paying job one day, a real job, you know?" He looked at Fred with raised eyebrows, then at Alice.

Fred nodded.

"A real job," Chet repeated, "a full-time, forty-hour-a-week job. That way I can make sure the kids are taken care of and finish school."

Fred tried to swallow the painful lump in his throat. "Is your father dead?"

Chet shook his head. "Naw. He's just out of work like so many other men these days. He's a good, hard worker," he was quick to say, "but the plant where he worked closed, and he hasn't been able to find another job. Been out of work over a year now."

"Like my friend Dot's father," Alice said.

Chet nodded. " 'Course, maybe Dad's found a job since I

57

left. Like I said, I haven't heard from them."

"If your father isn't dead and you like your family, why did you leave home?" Fred asked.

Chet didn't answer right away. He kept staring out at the street. Fred saw him swallow. He thought he saw a glint of tears in Chet's eyes, but then it was gone. *I must have imagined it,* he thought.

Finally Chet said, "One day my dad came home from looking for work. Like most days, he hadn't found a job and hadn't found any work for chores for a few hours, either. He was out of money, and the cupboards were empty. He took me aside and said, "You're the oldest, seventeen. You're not a boy anymore. I can't afford to feed everyone. It's time for you to be out on your own."

Alice gasped.

Fred stared. His chest felt cold with horror. *What if Father said that to me, just pushed me out of the house that way?*

"It wasn't his fault, of course," Chet said quickly. "I know he didn't want to do it." His shrug lifted his worn, dusty shirt. "He didn't have a choice. I knew that. We lived in a small town in western Minnesota, and I knew well enough there weren't any jobs to be had. So that night, I stuffed a change of clothes and a blanket and a razor into a pillowcase. I walked down to the train yard and caught a freight train headed east. That was the first time I rode the rails."

The clacking of Steven's wheels on the sidewalk made them all look up. Steven was flying toward them, his straight dark hair blowing. One foot pumped the sidewalk in a rhythm that kept his scooter moving fast over the cracks. A couple houses behind him, Isabel was still running, with Frank a couple houses behind her.

Steven waved at them. "Look at this! It works great!"

Chet grinned and waved back.

Relief loosened some of the tightness in Fred's chest. "I

think it must be exciting to live on the road like you do," he told Chet.

"It's interesting to see different places," he admitted, "but it isn't much fun wondering where you're going to sleep every night or whether you're going to have anything to eat that day and never having clean clothes."

"No, I guess not," Fred said slowly.

"Remember the pillowcase of stuff I told you I took with me from home?"

Fred nodded.

"Yes," Alice said. "What happened to it?"

"Someone stole it from me. Most of the hobos are gentlemen."

"I've heard that," Alice said, smiling. "They're called the Gentlemen of the Road."

Chet winked at her. "That's right. But hobos aren't the only ones riding the rails. Sometimes you meet up with a tough guy. That's what happened to me. He used to be in prison, and he didn't want to reform. He threatened me with a knife and told me he wanted the pillowcase and anything else I had."

Alice clapped a hand over her mouth.

Fred hugged his knees. "What did you do?"

Chet shrugged again and looked as calm as though he were explaining an arithmetic problem. "What *could* I do? I let him take it. I had fifty cents on me from a couple days' work, and he took that, too. So you see, it can be dangerous."

"But hobos usually become friends with each other, don't they?" Fred asked. "That's what I've heard. They look out for each other."

"In some ways they do, but you don't want to get too close to anyone on the road. Most stick to themselves. If you go to someone's house to ask for work, it scares people if there's more than one of you."

Alice nodded. "I guess it might be scary to see a bunch of strangers come to your door together."

"There are other reasons to stick to yourself, too," Chet said. Fred thought the other boy got a faraway look in his eyes.

"When I first started riding the rails, I met this kid about my age. His name was Ron. He and I got along like this." Chet held up two fingers, wrapped together.

"What happened?" Fred asked. "Did he go back home?"

"No." Chet was quiet for a minute. "One night, we caught a train outside a small town. We hid on top of the train as it left town, laying down so we couldn't be seen. But it's hard to hold on up there. Dangerous, too. Lots of hobos have been thrown off the top of trains when the trains went around corners. So we climbed down between two of the freight cars. On the back of cars there are iron handles, like a ladder built into the train car. We stood with our feet on one of the bottom handles and holding on to one of the high handles."

He stopped talking and just watched the street with that faraway look in his eyes again. Excitement built inside Fred, waiting for the end of Chet's story. He hugged his knees tighter.

"It was really cold that night," Chet said finally. "Between us, we had one pair of gloves. We were each wearing one glove because it's hard to hold on to cold iron with bare hands. I was on the back of one car, and Ron was on the back of the other, so our backs were to each other. Suddenly, there was a jerk. I almost lost my hold. I heard Ron yell. I glanced back and saw he was falling."

Chet reached out a hand. "I grabbed for him. I felt his hat against my knuckles. Then he was gone, just slipped under the wheels of that train. He died."

CHAPTER 9

The Closed Bank

Two days later, Fred was walking quickly in the cool October sunshine. He shivered, remembering Chet's story and the fate of his friend Ron. Fred hadn't been able to forget the story since Chet told it to them. He wanted to do something for Chet, and he thought he knew just the thing.

I'll loan him some money, he thought. *I have twelve dollars in my savings account. I'd rather loan it to Chet than keep it in the bank. Chet needs it more than I do.*

Fred hurried past an empty brick store. It used to be a clothing store, he remembered. Now its windows were dark and empty except for a sign someone had put on the window. "Hard times are still Hoovering over us," the sign said.

It seemed everyone was blaming President Hoover for the bad times. *Pretty soon he might not be president anymore,* Fred thought. *Maybe that other man, Franklin Roosevelt, will be president instead.*

He turned the corner of the business street and began walking faster. His bank was in the middle of the block, a big, brick building with tall, heavy glass doors.

He hurried the last few feet. In just a few minutes, he'd have his money in his pockets. In his mind, he could see Chet smiling and thanking him when he handed him the money. The thought brought a smile to his face as he reached the bank.

He pushed against the door.

It didn't move.

He pushed again. Still it didn't budge.

Surprised, he stood back and stared at the door. Inside, the bank was as dark as the abandoned store he'd passed earlier. On the inside of the door, someone had hung a sign. "Closed until further notice."

"Closed!" Fred stared. "It can't be."

A strange empty feeling filled the spot where his stomach should have been. "It can't be," he repeated in a whisper. He stood with his hands on the glass of the door, staring at the sign and the empty lobby inside.

Fred knew that banks could close. When they did, no one could take their money out of the bank or put money into it. It was like a store that went out of business. Lots of banks all over the country had closed in the last few years, hundreds of banks, thousands of banks. *But not my bank!*

Slowly he started for home. He stared at the sidewalk as he walked but didn't see it. A man passing by was whistling Franklin Roosevelt's campaign song, "Happy Days Are Here Again!"

Fred snorted. *What a joke that is!* he thought. He wouldn't be able to loan Chet any money. *I won't be able to spend my own money on anything. I feel like I've been robbed!*

"See you later, Martha," Alice said as Martha started down the hall toward her classroom.

Beside her, Dot shook her head. "I guess Mirna isn't in school today."

"No, I guess not." Sadness wound through Alice. She hated the way the depression was hurting so many of her friends.

She watched Martha until her faded dress was lost in the crowd of other students milling about the hallway waiting for school to start.

Martha and Mirna were twins. They were in the class ahead of Alice and Dot. Like Dot's father, their father had been out of work for a long time. Martha had told Alice a few weeks ago that they only had one dress left that fit both her and Mirna.

"We don't want to quit going to school," she'd said to Alice, "so we're going to take turns going. I'll go one day, and Mirna will go the next."

Alice had been stunned. Now she told Dot, "I guess it shouldn't be such a surprise about Martha and Mirna. Lots of kids aren't coming to school now."

Dot nodded. "Mother and Father say I will go to school no matter how poor we get. Sometimes it's embarrassing, though, wearing old clothes and shoes with holes in them."

"Lots of kids are wearing old clothes now," Alice comforted her. "And almost everyone wears cardboard in their shoes to cover the holes in the soles."

"At least I still have shoes to put cardboard inside of," Dot said. "The boys in one family in my neighborhood quit going to school because they don't have shoes. Their father says it's too cold in Minnesota to go without shoes this time of year. There are some charities and churches that give away old shoes, but their father says he doesn't want his family taking charity."

"Not even for his kids to have shoes?" The awfulness of it burned inside Alice's chest.

Dot shook her head. "No. My father doesn't like taking charity, either, but he thinks the boys' father should take the free shoes." She took a deep breath. "I can understand how Martha and Mirna feel, though. A couple years ago, I wouldn't have come to school without good clothes."

Alice knew that was true. When Dot's father had an important job that paid lots of money, Dot had worn some of the prettiest dresses in school. But he'd lost his job three years ago, and Dot had grown a lot since then. Most of her beautiful clothes didn't fit now. Many had been remade, but even those were faded and worn.

Alice grinned at her friend. "You were pretty uppity back then. I like you better now, even if your clothes aren't the best ones in town."

"Hi, Alice! Hi, Dot!" Fred stopped beside them. "Hey, Dot, Father came home last night with some jars of sauerkraut from the Organized Unemployed. The company Pastor Mecklenburg started must be doing pretty well."

A smile brightened Dot's face. "It's going swell!" She laughed. "A farmer gave them *twenty thousand* bushels of cabbage, so the company is making sauerkraut out of it to sell."

"Where do they make it?" Alice asked.

"At the old Central High School. The city is letting the company use it. A restaurant gave them kitchen equipment." Dot laughed again. "You wouldn't believe how bad that old school smells with all that cabbage and sauerkraut!"

Alice and Fred laughed with her.

"Is your father still working with the company?" Fred asked.

"Oh, yes! Pastor Mecklenburg says Father was a gift from God because he's such a good businessman."

Alice smiled. She could see how proud Alice was of her father.

"He's even being paid now." Dot shrugged. "In paper scrip, like everyone else, of course. We've used it to buy food, mostly. With that and the food we grew and canned this summer, we have lots of food now."

"Does your father like working there?" Alice asked.

Dot nodded. "He says that with the money the company is making from selling the sauerkraut, it's buying material and sewing machines. The company is going to make clothes and sell them, too. It's opening its own store to sell the things it makes."

Fred raised his eyebrows. "How do the men know how to make sauerkraut and sew? Not many men know how to cook and use sewing machines."

"Both men and women work at the company," Dot told him, "and there are *lots* of workers."

Alice jumped when the bell rang, warning them that classes would be starting in five minutes. Fred headed toward his class, and Dot and Alice walked toward theirs.

"I almost forgot to tell you." Dot's eyes sparkled. "Mother used some of the scrip to buy flour. She let me choose which bags. I chose some with pretty pink and blue and yellow flowers on them. She's going to make me a new dress with the bags."

"That's nice!" *A couple years ago, Dot would never have worn a dress made out of a flour sack,* Alice thought. *Of course now, lots of girls are doing that.*

The girls slipped into their wooden desks just as the final bell rang. Right away, Miss Atkins stood at the front of the class and greeted everyone with a smile. "Good morning, class. We're going to start today with our readers."

Alice dutifully opened her reader to the right page. As a girl on the other side of the room began reading aloud, Alice followed along.

After a page, Alice lost interest in the story. Her gaze slipped to Miss Atkins. The teacher was leaning against the front of her desk with a reader open in her hands. She was tall and very skinny. She had dark hair that she wore to the side with a ribbon. The ribbon always matched her dress. Today it was navy blue.

Alice looked out the window. She could hear other students reading, but she didn't pay attention. The branches outside the window were almost bare of leaves now that it was the end of October. A squirrel raced along one of the branches.

I wish I could be outside playing like you are, she told the squirrel silently. Guilt made her squirm and look back at her book.

Hundreds of schools, maybe thousands, had closed all over the country because cities and counties and states didn't have enough money to keep them open. Alice knew she should be glad she could still go to school. She'd heard a rumor that Minneapolis was running out of money to pay its teachers, too. She'd asked her father whether it was true and if her school would close. He'd said he didn't know.

"No, Harold," Miss Atkins told the boy who was reading, "that's not the way to pronounce hospital. Let me write it on the blackboard and we can all see how it should be spoken."

She walked to the board behind her desk and picked up a piece of chalk from the ledge. She wrote H, O, S, P—

The chalk made a squeaky sound that made Alice shiver. Instead of an I, a squiggly line went down the blackboard.

Then Miss Atkins fell to the floor.

For a moment, the room was as quiet as if no one was in it. No one moved. No one made a sound.

They waited for Miss Atkins to get up.

She didn't.

Chapter 10
What Happened to Miss Atkins?

Alice's heart started beating so hard that she could feel it hitting her chest. She pushed herself out of her desk and walked slowly to the front of the room. Miss Atkins was lying there with her eyes closed.

Alice knelt beside her and gently pushed at her shoulder. "Miss Atkins? Miss Atkins, wake up!"

A couple other students stood behind Alice. "Is she dead?" she heard one of the boys ask.

Alice shook her head. "She's still breathing."

Dot knelt beside her. Alice looked at her. Dot's green eyes were huge, and her face was white. She looked scared. *Do I look like that?* Alice wondered. *I sure feel scared.*

"What happened to her?" one of the other students asked.

Alice shook her head. "I don't know, but I think we'd better get the school nurse."

"I'll get her." Dot stood up and started for the door.

Alice looked back down at Miss Atkins. She really liked her teacher. *What's wrong with her?* she wondered.

Fear skittered along her nerves.

All day, Alice worried about Miss Atkins. The teacher had awakened before Dot returned with the school nurse, but the class still didn't know what was wrong with her. The nurse had sent Miss Atkins home, and the class had a substitute teacher for the rest of the day.

That evening, Fred's father, Uncle Richard, came over to Alice's house to talk with her. They sat down in the living room with Alice's parents.

"I'm Miss Atkins's doctor," Uncle Richard told Alice. "She came to see me today."

Alice scooted to the edge of the chair. "Is she okay?"

He nodded. "She'll be all right. Doctors aren't supposed to tell other people about their patients, but Miss Atkins asked me to let you know she is okay." He smiled. "She told me you were the student who thought of sending for the school nurse. That was very smart. It was just the right thing to do."

Happiness at his words and that Miss Atkins wasn't terribly ill filled Alice's chest. "Why did she fall on the floor and go to sleep like that?"

"She fainted."

"Why?"

Uncle Richard's face grew very serious beneath his black and gray hair. "She hasn't been eating enough."

Alice stared at him, surprised. "Why not? She has a job, so she can buy food. She doesn't have to stand in bread lines like homeless men."

"Miss Atkins is the only person in her family with a job," Alice's uncle explained. "She lives with her parents. So do her grandparents and her two younger sisters. Neither of her older brothers or their wives have jobs, and both brothers have children. Miss Atkins's pay has to buy food for everyone and pay all the other bills for everyone, too. There isn't enough money to go around. Your Miss Atkins is a very nice woman." He smiled at Alice.

Alice gave him a wobbly little smile back. She thought Miss Atkins was nice, too, but she didn't like it that her teacher was hungry.

"She is very nice," he repeated. "To make sure everyone else gets enough to eat, she skips eating meals herself. Usually she only eats one meal a day. Sometimes she doesn't eat at all."

"Oh." Alice tried to imagine what it was like not to eat anything all day. She got hungry just waiting for supper!

Uncle Richard held up a finger. "Don't forget, Alice, this is Miss Atkins's secret. You mustn't tell any of your friends."

"I won't," she said. "But I can tell Jesus and pray for her, can't I?"

"I'm sure Miss Atkins would like that very much."

Fred sat at the kitchen table, carefully telling his parents of his plan to give a loan to Chet and how the plan had fallen through when the bank closed.

His father frowned. "Did Chet *ask* you for this loan?"

Fred shook his head quickly. "Oh, no. He's never asked me for anything. He doesn't even know about my savings account. It was all my idea."

70

"It was nice of you to think of it," Mother said slowly.

Fred took a deep breath. What would his parents think of his new idea for helping Chet? "I was wondering, could Chet stay with us?"

Father and Mother looked at him with surprise in their eyes.

"Son," Father said, "what made you think of this?"

"Well, Chet doesn't have a place to stay."

"What about the Salvation Army, the Union Mission, and the other charities in town?" Father asked.

"Chet says those places only let a man stay there a few nights. They only let kids like Chet stay one night. They don't give the kids as many meals, either."

"Why not?" Mother's eyes looked troubled.

"Because they want the kids to go back to their parents' houses to stay," Fred explained. "But Chet can't go back because his father told him he had to leave." He quickly told them Chet's story. "So you see, he doesn't have a place to stay."

Father sat with his elbows on the table. He rubbed a hand over his chin, back and forth, while he thought.

Please say yes, Fred told him, silently. *Please let Chet stay.*

Mother watched Father. She didn't say anything.

Father lowered his hand with a sigh. "Fred, there are thousands of boys like Chet. Almost a quarter million of them are riding the rails, looking for work. Lots of them are younger than Chet. All of them are broke and hungry and don't have a roof over their heads most of the time. We can't help all of them."

"I'm not asking you to help all of them, only Chet. We have room. This is a big house."

"We won't have as much room in a couple days," Father said. "Larry and his wife are moving back home this weekend."

Fred's mouth dropped open. His oldest brother, Larry, hadn't lived at home since he graduated from the university. "They are?"

Father nodded. "You know he lost his job when the company where he worked closed. He hasn't been able to get another job yet and neither has his wife. They can't pay for their rent or their other bills."

Fear grew inside Fred, a fear he'd never known before. There were men all over the city who didn't have jobs and couldn't support themselves and their families. Even his older brother, Harry, could only find small jobs that lasted a day or two. But Harry hadn't graduated from the university, and he wasn't married. He'd always lived at home with Fred and their parents.

Larry was different. And it felt different when it was his brother that needed help. It felt. . .scary.

He didn't want to feel that way. He didn't want to think about it. He remembered Chet. "Isn't there *something* we can do to help Chet? Isn't there work you can give him?"

"Don't you think any work we could offer should first go to Harry or Larry?" Father's voice was low and quiet.

"I suppose." Fred knew Father was right, so why did the truth feel so awful?

The next evening when the Harringtons had listened to *Amos 'n' Andy* and then the news, Alice's father switched off the radio.

Alice took a deep breath. *Now is the time to ask,* she thought. She rubbed her sweaty hands down the sides of her dress.

Fred had told her at school that day about his conversation with his parents. "Why don't you ask your parents if they can help Chet?" he'd asked her. She'd promised him she would ask them that night.

Father was already settling onto the sofa and opening up

the newspaper. Mother was in her rocker beside the radio, mending the heel in one of Steven's socks.

Alice cleared her throat. "Um, Father? Mother? There's something I want to ask you."

Father lowered the newspaper. Mother looked up from her mending. They both smiled at her, waiting.

Her mouth was so dry it felt like it was sticking together. She swallowed hard. "Do you. . .do you think maybe Chet Strand could stay here?"

"What?" The word seemed to explode from Father's lips. Mother stared at her with her mouth open.

This is going to be worse than I thought, Alice thought. "Well, you know he's a hobo. He doesn't have any place to stay, and it's almost winter." She swallowed again. "Maybe, if he can't stay here, you could give him some work to do."

"Maybe we'd better tell her," Mother said to Father quietly.

"Tell me what?" Alice asked.

Father sighed. He folded the newspaper and set it beside him on the sofa. Then he leaned forward, resting his elbows on his knees. "The mill cut my hours today. I won't be making as much money as before."

Alice's stomach felt like she'd just drank a glass of sour milk. *Are we going to be poor?* she wondered.

"I don't know where we'd put Chet." Father spread his hands and smiled at Alice. "We have five children now. Where would we put Chet?"

Alice didn't smile back at him. "I guess we don't have room for another bed."

"There's another way it wouldn't be fair." Father's smile faded. "Our whole family is going to have to tighten their belts and watch what we spend. I don't know if it would be fair to Chet to let him live with us now, when we have to be so careful

73

with our money. I don't know if it would be fair to the rest of the family, either, to spend money on Chet. We will have to be careful with our money just to meet our own family's needs. Do you understand, Alice?"

She nodded. She still felt sick to her stomach. "Is your company going to close, Father? Are you going to lose your job?"

"I don't know, pumpkin. But that's not something for you to worry about. Worrying about taking care of you and the rest of the family is my job. Okay?"

Alice nodded again, but inside, she still worried. She knew lots of kids whose fathers' hours were cut. Then the men were working only a couple days a week, then only a couple days every other week, until the families had almost no money. Lots of the men ended up losing their jobs.

Is that going to happen to Father? Fear wormed its way into her heart.

CHAPTER 11
An Important Letter

"Make it last. Wear it out. Make do or do without." Alice dropped the sock she was mending into her lap. She glared at her mother, who sat beside her on the sofa. "I'm sick of hearing those words."

It had been six weeks since Father had told her about his hours being cut back. The family had been trying to find ways to spend less money ever since. Mother tried to make it a game. At first it seemed like fun. Now it was growing old.

To make things worse, last night Father had told the family his hours were cut back still farther.

Mother laid a hand on Alice's knee and smiled. "They are good words. Making the best use we can of everything we have is one way of showing God we're grateful for what He gives us. It shows Him we want to use the money He gives us wisely."

"I wish He'd just give us more money." Alice stuck her bottom lip out in a pout.

Mother laughed. "That wouldn't make us any wiser, would it?"

Alice supposed she should feel guilty for the way she felt, but she didn't. She stuck the needle into the heel of the sock. She didn't like mending socks. The mended places always felt thick and rough on her feet. Mother said the smaller and closer together the stitches were, the better the socks would feel when she wore them. But doing it right only made the mending harder. She jabbed the needle in again. "Ow!"

"Stick yourself?" Mother asked.

Alice stuck her thumb in her mouth to try to make it stop hurting. She blinked away the tears that had rushed to her eyes when the needle jabbed into her thumb.

"I wish this old depression would go away," she said when she took her thumb out of her mouth.

"So does everyone else, pumpkin."

"I don't know why everyone is so excited that Mr. Roosevelt was elected president last month. Nothing has gotten any better."

Mother laughed. "Why, he was just elected. He doesn't take office until next March. Mr. Hoover is still president until then."

"Oh. Why did God let this old depression happen, anyway? Why is He letting so many people go hungry and without jobs or homes? I thought God loved us."

Mother put down the sock of Father's she was mending and turned to face Alice. Her usually cheerful face was serious. "God does love us."

Alice stuck out her chin. She lifted her angry gaze to her mother's face. "Then why did the stock market crash and people lose their money and jobs?"

"Well, I'm not sure, but I think it's something like this." Mother settled against the back of the sofa. "You know what happens when someone breaks a law? For instance, what if someone is caught stealing?"

"He goes to jail."

"Right. What happens if we break one of God's laws, for instance, one of the Ten Commandments?"

"We have to ask Him to forgive us."

"Right. There are other laws, too. Laws besides God's laws and people's laws."

"Like what?"

"Like laws of nature. The law of gravity is a law of nature. And there are laws of money, too. They are usually called laws of economics. Before the stock market crash, people became greedy. They wanted to buy more things than they had money to pay for. They found ways to do that for a long time. But in the end, there wasn't enough money to pay for everything they had bought. They broke the laws that tell us how money works."

"Oh." Alice shook her head. "I don't think I understand. I've heard some people say God is punishing America for being greedy and for so many people breaking the law and drinking liquor and for other things people are doing wrong. Do you think God is punishing us?"

Mother slipped her arm around her shoulder. "I don't know. The only thing I know for sure is that all we can do is to live every day the way we think God wants us to, loving each other and trying to help each other. Maybe that will be the most important thing people learn from these hard times, to love and help each other. Wouldn't that be a good lesson?"

Alice nodded. "Yes. But if that's what God's doing, I wish the lesson were over."

"If that's the lesson," Mother said, "it won't be over until we learn it."

Fred and Alice ran into Chet a couple days later in the park. They greeted each other warmly, though there was a cold December wind blowing.

"Did you check with the Organized Unemployed to see if you could get a job with them?" Fred asked Chet. He and Alice had suggested it to Chet the last time they'd seen him. Alice had even told him to tell Dot's father he was a friend of theirs.

"Yeah. I talked to Mr. Lane like you told me to, but I can't work there. They don't hire kids, and they don't hire people who aren't from Minneapolis. They think it's more important to hire people from here and people who have families to take care of."

Frustration poured through Fred. "I'm sorry." Nothing he tried to do for Chet worked!

Chet shrugged. He stuffed his hands in his pockets and hunched against the cold wind. "It's all right. I understand why they have those rules. If someone with a family gets the job, the job helps a lot more people than if someone like me gets the job."

"I suppose." It didn't make Fred feel any better.

"Did you hear what Minneapolis's new mayor said about hobos?" Anger filled Chet's voice. His brown eyes flashed.

"What?" Alice asked.

"He called us 'floaters.' Says we're costing Minneapolis thirty cents a day to feed and give a place to sleep. He wants all the missions to stop helping hobos."

Fred's mouth dropped. "Why?"

"He thinks if the missions stop helping hobos, men without jobs will stop coming to Minneapolis."

"Will they?" Fred asked.

Chet shrugged again. "Some, probably. What the mayor doesn't seem to understand is that people are coming here because they can't find work in their hometowns. So why stay in their hometowns? And besides, people from Minneapolis who can't find work are going to other cities looking for work. The missions in the other cities help the people from Minneapolis. Why shouldn't Minneapolis help us?"

Fred and Alice exchanged troubled looks. *What if the mayor stops helping kids like Chet? If the missions won't help Chet and the other kids, and they can't go home, where will they go?*

Something wet landed on the tip of Fred's nose. He looked up. "It's starting to snow. Why don't you come home with me for supper, Chet?"

Chet pressed his lips together. "I don't know if I should. Your folks might not have any chores for me."

"Aw, there's always something that needs to be done." Fred hoped it was true. With Larry and Harry home and helping around the house and yard, and with patients offering help in return for his father's services, he wasn't sure what there might be to do.

"All right," Chet said. "A hot meal will taste good."

Fred's mother greeted Chet with a smile. "No, I don't have any chores that need to be done right now. But I was hoping we'd see you again soon. I was thinking of the little wooden bird you carved for Audrey. I'd like to give a couple to friends for Christmas. Would you be able to carve some for me?"

A grin filled Chet's face. "You bet!"

"Do you ever sell those, Chet?" Fred asked.

"Those little things? Naw. Who'd pay for them?"

"Sounds like Mother would pay for them."

"Of course I will," she said.

"I couldn't ask you to do that," Chet said. "You can have them in exchange for supper."

Excitement filled Fred. "Chet, with Christmas coming up, I bet you could sell lots of your carvings."

"That's a wonderful idea!" Mother agreed.

Chet's face lit up with hope. "You think so? Maybe I'll try it."

After supper, Fred was glad to hear his father say, "I think you should stay here tonight, Chet. Looks like we're going to get a good old-fashioned snowstorm."

Fred thought Chet's face looked older than his seventeen years. "Thank you, sir, but I couldn't do that. You've a full house."

"You can sleep on the sofa," Father said. "I hear the missions are overflowing with men, that they have to turn them away. This would be no night to spend outside. If my own boys were fending for themselves, I'd want them to have a warm place to sleep."

Chet's face grew sterner. "I don't want charity from you."

Father nodded. "I understand that. How about if you carve one of those birds my wife wants, and we trade? I take things in trade from my patients all the time. No reason we can't barter, too."

Chet was silent for a moment. Then he nodded. "That sounds fair. Thank you, sir."

A warm happiness spread through Fred. Finally his family was able to help Chet! At least a little bit.

The next day, Alice told Fred, "I've been thinking about what

Chet said. You know, about the mayor wanting people to stop helping the hobos. I think we should do something about it."

Fred snorted. "Like what? The mayor won't care what we think."

"He'll care what the newspaper says, won't he?"

"Maybe. So?"

"I think we should write a letter to the newspaper. The newspapers print letters people write to them, you know. We can write why we think people should keep helping hobos like Chet."

"I don't know if it will work," Fred said, "but if you want to try it, go ahead."

Alice bit her bottom lip. "I kind of hoped you would help me. It would be easier if we wrote it together."

"Well. . .okay."

Four days later, they saw their letter in the editorial column of the Minneapolis *Tribune*. Alice saw it first. She called Fred and told him to read it.

The next day, she was pleased and surprised when Miss Atkins read the letter to her class. Alice felt her face grow hot when other students turned to look at her, and she knew she was blushing.

"Why don't you come to the front of the room," Miss Atkins asked Alice when she was done reading the letter, "and tell us why you wrote the letter?"

Alice went to the front as she was asked. She clasped her hands behind her back to try to keep from feeling so nervous. Then she told them about meeting Chet, how he had to leave home because his father couldn't take care of everyone in his family, and how hard it was for Chet to find work and food and a place to sleep.

When she was done, Miss Atkins asked the class whether

they agreed with Alice or with the mayor. Alice was glad to see most of them agreed with her. She was even more glad when Miss Atkins gave the class the assignment of writing to the mayor to tell them what they thought he should do and why.

Alice and Dot headed toward Dot's home after school. They were so interested in talking about Chet and the letter and what happened in school, that Dot forgot to ask Alice not to come into her house. They walked in together, talking fast to each other.

From the hallway of Dot's home, Alice stared at the living room. It was empty.

CHAPTER 12
Christmas Plans

"What happened to your furniture, Dot?" Alice asked.

All the color seemed to drain from Dot's face. Tears glittered in her eyes. "I didn't want you to know."

A chill ran through Alice. Something was terribly wrong. "Know what? Are you moving?"

Dot shook her head. "We've been selling our furniture to pay for the house."

"But I thought the house belonged to you. You don't rent it."

"There's a mortgage on the house," Dot said.

Alice frowned. "I've heard that word before, but I don't know what it means."

"It means that Father borrowed money from the bank to

buy the house. The loan the bank gave him is called a mort-gage. Then he paid the money the bank gave him to the man who owned the house before us. Now Father has to pay the bank for the money he borrowed. He has to pay some every month, like people pay rent. And we don't have enough money to pay it."

"Oh." Alice looked at the almost empty room. "But I thought things were better now that your father is working for Organized Unemployed."

"They are. But we've spent all the money Father had saved when he lost his job. The bank won't take scrip for the mort-gage. So we started selling anything we could to pay it." Dot sighed. "We keep hoping Father will find a real job that pays money and not just scrip before the bank takes our house away."

Alice stared at her friend in horror. "The bank can't do that, can it?"

Dot changed the subject, but Alice wasn't listening. All she could think was, *What if the bank takes Dot's house? What if Dot's family has to live without a home, like Chet?*

The next day was Friday. Alice's mother said she could ask Dot and Fred to join them for supper. After they ate, Steven and Isabel played fox and geese with them in the snow outside. When they came back in, Steven and Isabel went into the liv-ing room to play. Alice and Dot and Fred talked in the kitchen while they made hot chocolate.

They carried mugs of hot chocolate to the kitchen table. Dot sighed when she sat down. "Christmas is only a couple weeks away."

Alice grinned. "I know. I can hardly wait."

Fred blew over the top of his mug to cool his chocolate. "I've been trying to sell Christmas Seals, but people aren't buying them like they used to do. Not many people seem to have money to spend on Christmas Seals this year."

"I know we don't," Dot said. She sighed again. "I don't even have money to buy presents for Mother and Father or the nieces and nephews who are living with us."

"I don't have much money to buy presents for my family, either," Alice said. "Maybe we can make presents."

"Like what?" Dot asked.

Alice shrugged. "I don't know. Chet carves birds and animals out of wood."

Dot laughed. "I can't do that."

"I helped Chet make a scooter for Steven," Fred said. "There's another skate left from the pair Chet used. I could make a scooter for your nephew, Dot."

"Would you?" Dot's face lit up.

"Sure. It would be fun."

Dot's shoulders sagged. "I don't have anything to pay you."

Fred shrugged. "You don't need to pay me. We're friends."

"Gifts are nice," Dot told him, "but when people give you things because you can't pay for them, it's not a gift, it's charity."

"What's the difference?" Alice asked.

"Yeah. I'd be making the scooter because we're friends."

"There's a big difference," Dot said. "Gifts make you feel good. Charity makes you feel bad, like you can't take care of yourself."

"Oh." Alice thought it made sense when Dot explained it.

Fred crossed his arms on the table. "Well, then, we'll just find something you can do to pay for it."

"Like what?" Dot asked.

"I don't know," Fred said. "We'll think about it. Something will come up."

"I know what I want to make for my brothers and sisters," Alice said. "At least, for everyone but Audrey. She's too small for it."

"What?" Dot asked.

"I'm going to make jigsaw puzzles for them."

"How are you going to do that?" Fred asked.

"Simple," Alice said. "I'm going to ask Mother if I can have some of her old magazines. Then I'm going to find pictures I think Steven and Isabel and Frank will like. I'll cut out the pictures and paste them on a piece of cardboard. Then I'll cut the cardboard into pieces to make a puzzle." She held out her hands. "See? It's simple."

"I could do that for my nieces, too," Dot said eagerly. "It wouldn't cost anything!"

Alice grinned, feeling happy she'd found a way to help Dot. "We could cut out pictures to make calendars for our mothers and fathers, too."

"That's a great idea! I can do that, too," Fred said.

Alice leaned back in her chair. Some of her happiness seeped away. "I forgot. Isabel wants a play stove for Christmas. I wanted to buy it for her."

Fred wiggled his eyebrows. His blue eyes danced. "Your father hired Chet to make one for her. He's working on it in our garage so she won't find it before Christmas. He's making it out of wood, and he's painting burners on top of it."

Dot laughed. "That's great. Isabel gets her stove, and Chet gets a job."

Alice slipped off her chair and carried her empty mug to the counter. "I'm going to ask Mom right now if we can have her old magazines."

"Great!" Fred said. "Then we can get started on the gifts right away."

Alice was filled with happiness as she went to the living room to talk with her mother. *It feels good to have a way to make our presents. I'm glad Dot can give her family presents, too.*

CHAPTER 13
Champion Bakers

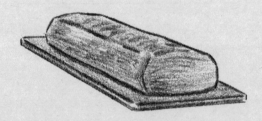

A couple days after Christmas, Dot came over to Alice's house.

"My family loved their presents!" she told Alice.

Alice grinned. "So did mine."

She took Dot into the living room and pointed. "See?" Steven and Isabel were putting together their puzzles.

The girls went up to Alice's room, where they could visit together without Alice's brothers and sisters around.

"Look what I got from Mother and Father," Alice said. She handed Dot a book.

"Nancy Drew! Wow, I wish I had a Nancy Drew book."

"You can read it when I'm done."

"Thanks!"

Alice flopped down on her bed. "We did a great job with our Christmas presents, didn't we?"

Dot sat on the edge of the bed, opening the book. "Uh-huh."

"Maybe we can come up with other good ideas. Like, maybe, how your family can make more money."

Dot looked up, her green eyes large. "Do you think so?"

"I don't know, but we could try. Let's come up with as many ideas as we can. They won't all work, but maybe one or two will help a little bit."

"Okay." Dot set the book on the bed beside her.

"Let's see." Alice rested her chin on the palm of her hand. "You could become a bank robber, but so many banks have closed that it wouldn't be worth the trouble."

Dot laughed. She put a hand behind her head and lifted her chin. "I could become a movie star."

Alice rolled her eyes. "Except you'd have to pay to go to Hollywood first."

"No I wouldn't. I could ride the rails like Chet."

"Maybe you could catch fish in the Mississippi River," Dot said. "Then you could cook them and sell fish sandwiches."

Dot wrinkled her nose. "I'd rather be a movie star, thank you."

Alice picked up the Nancy Drew book. "I know! You can be a detective!"

"Or I could write books. I know! I could write a book about two girls in Minneapolis who are best friends, Dot and Alice, and they solve all the mysteries the police can't solve."

The girls collapsed in a fit of giggles.

When they finally caught their breath, Dot said, "We need to think of something we can really do or sell."

"It's too bad you can't make things like Chet."

"Did he sell many of his carvings for Christmas?"

"Quite a few," Alice told her. "Of course, he had to take time to carve them first. He went house to house to sell them.

Sometimes he'd stand on street corners downtown and sell them there to the Christmas shoppers."

"That was a good idea. Is he still selling them?"

"He's trying, but not many people are buying them now that Christmas is over. Oh, I almost forgot to tell you. Chet's helping at a soup kitchen, too."

"He is?"

Alice nodded. "Aunt Frances, Fred's mother, helps at a soup kitchen, you know. One day Chet found out she was going down there to work and asked if he could go along. He said he'd never thought of helping at one of them before. After he went with Aunt Frances, he told the people at the kitchen that he'd like to help any time he needs to eat there. So the people in charge said he could."

"I can understand why he'd want to help there," Dot said. "That way it would be like he was working for his food instead of taking charity."

"That's what Chet said. Father says it shows what a good, responsible person Chet is."

"Where is Chet staying now?" Dot asked.

"When he can't find another place to stay, he stays at Fred's house. Fred says Chet is keeping a list of how many nights he stays there and how many meals he eats. Chet told Uncle Richard that when he finds a job, even if it's when he's real old, he's going to pay Uncle Richard back for everything. Chet still spends most days looking for work or selling his carvings."

"At least the mayor stopped trying to get missions to stop helping hobos like Chet," Dot said. "That was a good idea you had, writing to the newspaper."

They were quiet for a few minutes, both trying to think up something else for Dot to try.

"What about baking things?" Alice asked.

"Mother and I thought of that. Mother said she didn't think people who can hardly afford bread would want to spend their money on baked goods."

"No, I suppose not." Alice thought a minute longer. "What about baking bread, then? People can buy it in the stores for nine cents a loaf. If you sold it for seven or eight cents a loaf, maybe they'd buy it from you instead."

Dot sat up. Her face was filled with excitement. "That's a great idea!" Then her mouth drooped. "Except I don't think Mother could afford to buy all the ingredients to make enough bread to sell. I know we don't have enough in the house right now."

"Maybe Mother would loan you the ingredients, or Father might loan you the money for the ingredients."

"What if we couldn't pay it back?" Dot asked. "Then my parents would be upset."

"Well, maybe we should ask my mother if we can bake a few loaves. We can try to sell them. If it works, then maybe you and your mother could borrow the ingredients to make more from my mother. After you sold the bread, you could pay my mother back."

Dot brightened again. "Like a loan. That might work."

They hurried downstairs and asked Alice's mother.

"I think that's a great idea," Mother said. "You're welcome to use what we have, as long as you leave us at least one loaf of your bread until we can buy more for the family. You can use our kitchen to bake the bread."

Mother's aprons were huge. The girls had to fold them up around the waist and wrap the ties around them more than once.

When they'd mixed the dough and the loaves were set along the counter in a row beneath dishtowels to rise, Alice said, "It's a good thing it's Christmas vacation and we don't have to go to school. Making bread takes a long time!"

The kitchen smelled wonderful when the bread baked. "I wish we could eat it instead of sell it," Dot said grinning.

Hours after they'd started, when the loaves were baked and cooled, they put the loaves in baskets. Covering the baskets with clean dishtowels, they went house to house, offering the bread.

It was a little discouraging. Not everyone bought the bread. One woman even said, "Are you kidding? I make my own. Doesn't everyone?"

"I didn't think of that," Dot said as they left the woman's house. "I guess lots of people make their own instead of buying it at the store."

"Not everyone does, or the stores wouldn't sell it," Alice reminded her.

Finally they sold their last loaf. Walking up the steps to Alice's house, Alice said, "I didn't know making and selling bread would make my arms and feet so tired!"

Dot shook the small purse they'd brought along for the money. The coins in it jingled merrily. She grinned. "I don't feel so tired when I hear that sound."

"How did it go?" Mother asked when they entered the kitchen.

"Good," Alice told her. "We sold it all."

Mother looked at the empty baskets. "So you did. How much did people pay?"

"Most people paid eight cents a loaf," Dot said, "but at the end, if people said no, we offered it for seven cents instead. Then the bread sold faster."

Dot poured the coins out on the kitchen table. They made a satisfying noise as they piled up.

While the girls counted the coins, Mother made a list of all the supplies they'd used to make the bread and how much the supplies cost. When they were done, they compared the cost of the bread to the amount of money they had made.

"We made fifteen cents!" Dot's face glowed with excitement. "If Mother and I sold bread, and we made that much every time, it would really help my family!"

"Do you think your mother will try it?" Alice asked.

"I think she will if we can afford to buy the ingredients. Maybe we can use the scrip Father makes from Organized Unemployed to buy enough to make the first batch."

"If not," Mother told her, "we will loan you enough to buy the ingredients. Your mother can pay us back some each time you sell a batch. It wouldn't take long to repay."

Dot beamed. "Thanks. I think I'll go home right away and ask her about it."

Please let Dot's mother say yes, Alice prayed silently as she watched Dot hurry away down the sidewalk.

Dot's mother did say yes. "Well, what she really said is that we could try it," Dot reported with sparkling eyes to Alice and her mother the next day.

The bread project went great. Dot and her mother and her aunt made the bread and sold it door to door like Dot and Alice had done. They sold the bread all of January. Then in February, Dot came to school one morning with tears in her eyes.

"Even with the bread sales, we don't make enough to pay our whole monthly mortgage payment," she told Alice, as they stood in a corner of the hallway, where the other students wouldn't see her cry. "Yesterday the bank told Father that if he doesn't pay more money on the mortgage, the bank will take our house away at the end of the month."

Anger and frustration flowed through Alice in hot waves. *How could this happen? Why doesn't somebody fix all the things that are wrong in the country so my friends don't have to leave their homes?*

CHAPTER 14
A New President

Every day of February that passed without Dot's father getting a better job made Alice feel worse. She was frightened for her friend.

"At least we found one more way to save money," Dot said, wiping at the tears that streaked her face. "The Salvation Army gives milk to kids, so my nieces and nephews and I go every day with our tin pails. It's kind of embarrassing, but it tastes good."

Sometimes, it seems like I'm sad or scared all the time now, Alice thought as she and Fred walked into her house after school that day in late February. She felt especially bad because Dot had told her that tomorrow the bank would take their house.

Her father wasn't working today. Alice could hear him talking to Mother in the kitchen. "He's home a lot lately," she whispered to Fred in the hallway while they hung up their coats. "The company keeps cutting back his hours."

"My father's hours aren't cut back," Fred said, "but he says there're more patients every week who can't pay him. We've had to become more careful about money."

Alice nodded. "We have, too. Mother keeps trying to find new ways to save money."

They stopped talking to listen to her parents. Father's voice sounded sad.

It seems like all the adults I know seem unhappy and frightened most of the time, Alice thought, *just like me.*

"It seems like everything keeps getting worse," her father was saying. "The number of families receiving aid from the city has doubled in the last few months. Doubled!"

Mother sighed. "And we know there are lots of families that qualify for help who aren't asking for it. Families like Dot's."

"It's a good thing Richard and Frances let Chet stay with them when he will," Father said. "The city's been threatening to close their missions. They say there isn't enough money to keep them open."

Alice and Fred stared at each other, their eyes wide.

"If the missions close, what will all those homeless men do?" Alice whispered to Fred.

Fred held out his hands and shook his head. "I don't know."

Alice heard a chair scrape on the linoleum in the kitchen. Then Father said, "There's still worry over whether the city will have to close the schools soon, too. I'd sure hate to see that happen."

Alice and Fred exchanged scared looks. Then they walked into the kitchen.

"Do you really think the schools will close, Uncle Donald?" Fred asked as he and Alice sat down at the kitchen table across from him.

"Oh, hi, kids." Father pushed a hand through his curly hair. "I hope they won't, but the city is having a hard time paying all its bills. With so many people out of work, the city can't raise money very easily."

Mother set a glass of milk in front of Alice and one in front of Fred. She smiled at them. "I suppose you two would think it fun to have school close."

Fred grinned. "Maybe for a few days."

"It would be nice to have a vacation," Alice said, "but I don't think I'd like it if I knew I couldn't go back to school. If school stayed closed, how could anyone graduate?"

"They couldn't," Father said.

"If we don't graduate, we'll never be able to go to the university, will we?" Fred asked.

Father shook his head. "No."

"I don't know what I want to be yet," Fred said, "but I know I want to go to the university like Larry did."

"Dot wants to go to the university, too," Alice told him. "Or some school where she can learn to be a teacher."

"I didn't know she wanted to be a teacher," Mother said. "I think she'd be good at that. She likes children, and they like her."

Alice nodded. "There're some kids younger than us who live near her. Their father doesn't let them go to school. Dot uses her schoolbooks to help them learn their arithmetic and reading."

Mother smiled. "How nice of her!" She reached for the newspaper lying on the counter. "I almost forgot to tell you. There's good news today for Dot's family."

"What?" Alice asked. "They could sure use some good news!"

Mother laid the folded newspaper in front of her and pointed at a headline. "Governor Olson has stopped all fore-closures in Minnesota."

Alice frowned. "What's a foreclosure?"

"That's when a bank takes back a house because the people can't pay for their loan," Father explained.

Alice stared at him, scarcely daring to believe what her parents were saying. "You mean, Dot and her family get to keep their house?"

Mother smiled. "That's right."

"At least for a while," Father said. "Of course, one day Mr. Lane will have to pay the bank all the money he owes for the house. But for now, the bank won't be able to take it away."

Happiness flooded through Alice like a river. She grinned so wide her face hurt.

Fred pounded her on the back. A grin filled his face, too. "How about that for good news, cousin?"

"It's the best news I've had in my whole life," she told him.

On Saturday, Alice's family went over to Fred's house for dinner. It was an important day. Franklin Roosevelt was going to take the oath that would make him president.

While they waited in the living room, Fred's father shook his head. "The country's in such a mess, I can't imagine what FDR can do to help it out, but I hope he thinks of something!"

FDR was what a lot of people called the new president. They were the initials for his name, Franklin Delano Roosevelt.

"Things can't get much worse," Alice's father said, "no matter what FDR does. Since he was elected last November, everything's gotten worse under Hoover."

"Can't deny that," Fred's father agreed. "Stock market closed again today. Thirty-eight states have closed all their banks." He shook his head.

Thirty-eight states! Fred stared at his father, stunned. *All the people in those states who have money in banks must feel as awful as I felt when my bank closed.*

Finally the inauguration ceremony began. The families listened to the music and to the oath FDR took as the new president. Then it was time for FDR to give his first speech as president of the United States.

"First of all," the president's voice said over the radio in a strong, clear tone, "let me assert my belief that the only thing we have to fear is fear itself."

The only thing we have to fear is fear itself? Is that true? Fred wondered. *With all the people out of work and all the businesses that are closed and only ten states left that have banks open? It seems to me we have lots of things to be afraid of.*

President Hoover had tried to make business and banks better, to keep them open so people's jobs and money were safe. He hadn't been able to do it. Nothing he tried worked. Could this new man do anything to make things better?

Fred forced himself to listen to what FDR was saying. He was talking about the country, saying it had to move together, "as a trained and loyal army willing to sacrifice for the good of a common discipline."

When the speech was over, the families listened to another program. Fred was glad Will Rogers was on the radio. Father said Will Rogers was one of the wisest men in America. Fred just thought Will Rogers made true things sound funny, and Fred liked to laugh. He leaned forward when Rogers started to speak.

"America hasn't been as happy in three years as it is today,"

Will Rogers said. "No money, no banks, no work, no nothing; but they know they got a man in there who is wise to Congress and wise to our so-called big men. The whole country is with him, just so he does something. Even if what he does is wrong, they are with him. Just so he does something. If he burned down the Capitol, we would cheer and say, 'Well, we at least got a fire started anyhow.' "

The family was still laughing over what Rogers had said when Fred's father turned off the radio. "I think almost everyone in the country is willing to work together to get the country on its feet again," he said, "but I wonder what kinds of sacrifices FDR is going to ask of us."

The next day, they began to find out.

CHAPTER 15
A New Start

The next day, FDR called a national bank holiday and closed all the banks in the country. When Fred heard the news, fear slithered through him.

"Not one bank open in the whole country! What are people going to do to get money?" he asked his father.

"It's not as bad as it sounds," Father told him. "Lots of people believe that one of the reasons for the depression is problems with the banks. FDR is closing the banks so the problems can be fixed. He has a group of experts who will be working to solve the problems. Then the banks will open again."

"How soon until they open again?" Fred asked.

Father shook his head. "I don't know. No one knows. When the experts think they've fixed the problems, I guess."

Father's words didn't make Fred feel any better. Fred just felt sick to his stomach every time he thought about the banks being closed.

His stomach felt worse in church a week later when the offering plate was passed. There was only a little money in the plate when it came to him. There were a lot of IOU notes in it.

The banks weren't the only thing in the news. The German government had given some man named Adolph Hitler power over their country. Fred heard a few people at church say they didn't like that, but most people felt like one old man Fred overheard.

"We can't be troubling ourselves about other countries' problems," the old man said. "We need to fix our own country before we'll be strong enough to help any other countries."

Fred wasn't at all sure the United States could fix the depression.

The Harringtons and the Allertons had started getting together every Sunday. They'd share meals and talk and sometimes play games. Always they ended up listening to the radio after supper.

On March 12, the Sunday a week after the inauguration, FDR came on the radio to talk to the country again. He said this would be the first of what he called "fireside chats," where he would talk to the country on the radio every Sunday night. He wanted to let the country know what he was trying to do to make things better. He wanted to know what people thought he should do, too. He invited everyone who wanted to write to him and his wife.

One of the things FDR talked about during his first fireside chat was the banks. Fred shushed Alice's little brothers and sisters, who were playing in the middle of the Allertons' living room. "I want to hear this," he told them.

"Some of our bankers," the president said, "had shown themselves either incompetent or dishonest in their handling of the people's funds. They had used the money entrusted to them in speculations and unwise loans. . . . It was the government's job to straighten out this situation and to do it as quickly as possible. And the job is being performed."

"That's just what you said, Father," Fred whispered, "that he was trying to fix the bank problems."

Father nodded but didn't say anything. Fred could tell he was trying to hear the radio, so Fred listened, too. The next news was good: Banks in the twelve largest cities in the United States were going to open the next day!

"Are we one of the twelve largest cities?" Alice asked.

"No," her father said, "but we're close. If the banks in those other cities are opening, the banks here will open soon."

Fred and Alice grinned at each other. Fred felt like a rock had rolled off his chest. He'd been worried about those closed banks!

FDR told the people he'd asked Congress for money to help the banks. Congress agreed to give it to the banks, but the money was going to have to come from somewhere. Congress and FDR had decided they would get the money from two places: from money that was supposed to go to people who worked for the federal government and from veterans.

"Oh, no." Alice's mother's eyes looked troubled. "Not

from veterans! One of the reasons I voted for FDR is because I didn't like the way Hoover treated the veterans. Now FDR is taking money from them, too!"

"At least he's trying to help the banks," Fred's father said.

Alice's mother sighed. "I suppose so. There's only so much money to go around. I guess he has to take it from somewhere."

On his fireside chat the next Sunday night, the president told the country he'd sent a bill to Congress to help the farmers. It was called the Agricultural Adjustment Act, or the AAA.

On the next fireside chat, he told them he'd sent a bill to Congress to help unemployment. It was called the Emergency Work Act, or the ECW. He'd also signed a bill making the sale and drinking of beer legal again.

"Oh, dear!" Fred's mother held her hands to her face. "That's the first time any liquor has been legal since Prohibition became law in 1920."

Fred knew his mother had fought hard for Prohibition. She believed it wasn't good for children when their parents drank.

"FDR says the new law will make new jobs," Fred's father reminded her. "He's probably right."

Mother sighed. "I suppose so, but I still don't think the new law will be good for children."

"The city is like a new place, isn't it?" Chet said as he and Fred walked along one of the downtown streets together. "It used to feel like the city was asleep. No one seemed to have any hope things could get better. Now the city is jumping."

Fred nodded. "It sure is."

They had to move out into the street to walk around the next building. Wood was stacked on the sidewalk. A scaffolding covered the lower part of the store. A man stood on it, painting. Fred recognized the store. It had been empty a long time.

"Looks like this is going to be another saloon," Chet said.

They'd passed a number of other buildings that were being cleaned up. Most of them were going to be used for selling beer. The law said people could begin selling it next month.

"I guess FDR was right," Chet said. "The new beer law is going to make a lot of new jobs. The factories in town that make beer are already hiring people. They want to have beer ready to sell when the law starts. Men are sleeping outside the breweries, hoping to be the first in line when they hire people."

"Are you going to try to get one of the new jobs?" Fred asked.

Chet kicked at a stone. "Naw. I have an uncle who's a drunk. It really hurts his family. I don't want a job making something that hurts people."

Fred nodded. "That's what Dot's father said, too."

"Even if I wanted to work making beer, I probably couldn't get a job. Most jobs are still being given to men who have families to take care of."

They walked on a little farther. "It's my birthday today," Chet said quietly.

Fred stared at him in surprise. "It is? How old are you?"

"Eighteen. Maybe I'll be able to get more jobs now. Maybe employers won't keep thinking I'm such a kid."

Fred didn't answer. He didn't know what to say. Finally he said, "Maybe Mother will make a birthday cake for you."

Chet's cheeks flushed. He pulled the visor of his cap down almost to his eyebrows. "Naw. Birthday cakes are for kids."

Fred was pretty sure Chet would really like to have Mother make him a cake, but he didn't push it.

Everywhere they went, people seemed in good moods. One worker who was putting new glass in a store window was singing the FDR song. Fred and Chet found themselves humming along:

Happy days are here again!
  The skies above are clear again!
Let's all sing a song of cheer again—
  Happy days are here again!

Fred wasn't sure he believed the words, but he found his step had a bounce to it that hadn't been there before. "Are you staying at our place tonight?" he asked Chet.

"Naw." The older boy spread his hands, looked up at the sunny sky, and grinned. "Spring is almost here!"

Fred knew what that meant. With nicer weather, Chet wasn't so worried about finding a place to sleep. If he couldn't stay at one of the missions, he'd sleep outside—probably in one of the hobo jungles. That way he wouldn't feel guilty about staying in a bed he couldn't pay for.

Fred gave Chet a friendly poke with his elbow. "I was getting kind of used to having you around."

"Think I'll be leaving town in a couple days," Chet told him. "Might check out some farms and see if I can help some farmers get ready for spring."

A sudden pain flashed through Fred's chest. He'd miss his friend, but he knew Chet had to go.

The next day at supper, Father told Fred, "The president signed the employment bill yesterday, the Emergency Conservation Work Act. Remember him talking about that on his fireside chat?"

Fred nodded.

"Part of the new law was made just to help boys like Chet," Father continued. "It's called the Civilian Conservation Corps, or CCC."

"How's it going to help them?" Fred asked.

"The boys will be sent to work in places like the forests in northern Minnesota. They'll live together in camps like soldiers. They'll be paid thirty dollars a month, but they have to send twenty-five dollars home to their families each month. Since the government will give them a place to stay and food and clothes, the five dollars a month they get to keep should be more than enough for what they need."

Excitement rushed through Fred's chest. "It sounds perfect for Chet!"

Father shook his head. "The only problem is, it's only open to young men ages eighteen to twenty-five."

"But Chet just turned eighteen yesterday!"

Father grinned. "Then I agree with you. It sounds perfect for Chet."

Fred slumped against the back of his chair. "The only problem is, Chet's leaving town. He told me he's not going to stay here anymore. He's planning to go out in the country and try to find work on farms."

"That's too bad. Only 250,000 men will be admitted into the CCC, all over the country. And they can begin enrolling within the next couple weeks. I'd sure hate to see him miss out on this chance."

Fred couldn't stop thinking about Chet and the CCC. *I've got to find a way to tell him about this before he leaves the city!* he thought. *But how?*

While his parents and brothers listened to *Amos 'n' Andy,* Fred slipped into the hallway. Quietly he took his jacket and hat from the closet. *If Mother and Father hear me,* he thought, *they'll stop me.* He held his breath while he stole down the hall, into the kitchen, and out the back door.

CHAPTER 16
The Search for Chet

Standing on the back porch, Fred breathed in the cool night air and wondered, *Where should I start? The missions. Maybe Chet's staying at a mission tonight.*

A few blocks from home, he caught a trolley. He got off one block from the mission he knew Chet liked best. When he asked the people in charge whether they'd seen Chet, they shook their heads. "No, not tonight."

Fred thanked them, caught another trolley, and went to the Union City Mission. He got the same answer.

He got the same answer at the Salvation Army, too.

He didn't know what other mission to try, so he decided to

try the train station. His heart raced as he got off the trolley at the station. Maybe Chet was trying to catch a train out of the city right now! Maybe it was already too late, and Chet was already riding the rails into the countryside.

He went into the huge station. Even at night, it was filled with people leaving the city, arriving on trains, or waiting for people who were leaving or coming.

He went outside, slipping into the train yard where the trains left the depot. Watching carefully for the railroad bulls, he slipped through the edge of the yard. Here, hobos waited in the shadows, hoping to catch a ride before the trains began moving too fast. He asked a couple hobos whether they'd seen Chet. No one had.

Finally he gave up. There was only one place left to try. The hobo jungles.

Just thinking about it sent a chill down his spine. He'd heard awful tales about the jungles. His parents had told him to never, *never* go to a jungle. "But I have to find Chet," he whispered into the night, "and I don't know where else to go."

He knew where some of the jungles were. There was one along the Mississippi River, not far from the station. He decided to head there first.

Near the edge of the jungle camp, Fred stood behind a leafless bush. Through the branches, he could see a fire. Over the fire hung a large kettle. Fred could smell the jungle stew that cooked in the kettle. Men were sitting about the fire on the ground and on logs. Some of them were eating from tin cans. There was a large barrel a few yards away with another fire in it. A few men and boys stood around it, warming themselves against the cool spring air. Fred could hear men's voices as they visited together, but he couldn't tell what anyone was saying.

Fred searched the faces he could see in the firelight. He

couldn't see Chet. But maybe Chet was sitting or sleeping in the darkness beyond the light of the fires. *Even if he isn't here, maybe someone can tell me where he is.*

What would the men say when he walked into the jungle? Fred took a deep breath and stepped out from behind the bush.

His heart beat so hard he could feel it in his ears as he walked through the jungle to the fire where the kettle of stew gave off its aroma. He could tell the men and boys in the jungle knew he was a stranger here. As he neared the fire, people stopped talking and watched him.

His throat went dry. His hands started sweating. He'd never been so scared in his life!

He couldn't forget the warnings his parents had given him to stay away from the jungles. *Chet's a hobo, too,* he reminded himself silently. *He said most of the hobos he's met are nice.*

Fred tried to look at everyone while he walked, searching for Chet. He glanced out of the corner of his eye at a man in a torn coat and battered hat who was watching him. He remembered the man who had stolen from Chet. *There's always a few to watch out for,* he told himself, *like there's always a bully in every school class.* Fred made himself walk slow and easy, like he wasn't scared. *I hope I don't run into the jungle's bully,* he thought. He felt sweat running down his back.

He stopped at the fire.

One of the men stood up. "You can't have any stew unless you brought something to put in it."

Fred swallowed hard. "I. . .I didn't come for stew. I'm looking for someone, a friend."

A man sitting on the other side of the fire pushed his hat back on his head. "This friend got a name?"

"Chet. Chet Strand."

"Don't know him," the guy sitting down said.

"I don't know him, either," said the man who was standing.

Fred looked at the other men around the fire. "Do. . .do any of you know Chet?"

No one said anything.

Fred swallowed hard again. "Maybe you don't know him by name." He told them what Chet looked like.

No one said anything.

Fred took a couple steps backward. "Well, thank you." He turned around and started walking away. He was more frightened now than when he came into the jungle! The men were so unfriendly, like they were mad he walked into their jungle.

"Hey!" A man with a scraggly gray and black beard nodded at him.

Fred stopped. He hoped the man couldn't see him shaking.

"Why do you want to find this feller?"

"Um, I have some news for him that might help him get work."

"I know where you might find him."

"You do?" Hope pushed some of Fred's fear away.

"There's another jungle he stays at sometimes. It's about a mile from here."

"Can you tell me how to get there?"

"Sure." The man started giving him directions.

Fred listened carefully. He didn't want to have to ask the man to repeat himself.

Suddenly someone grabbed his arm. Fred's heart leaped into his throat!

"What are you doing here, Fred?"

"Chet!" Fred thought his legs would melt from relief.

Chet was scowling at him. "Yeah, it's me. Why are you here?"

"I was looking for you."

"C'mon. Let's go where we can talk." Chet led the way out of the jungle and up onto a sidewalk. Streetlights with five round bulbs spread welcome light. Fred's fear disappeared. He grinned at Chet. "I was beginning to think I'd never find you."

Chet didn't grin back. "How could you have been so foolish? Jungles can be dangerous places."

"But—"

"You aren't looking for me 'cause you're planning to run away from home are ya? 'Cause if you are, I'm not going to have anything to do with it."

"I—"

"When a boy has a family as fine as yours, a family that can afford to keep him at home, he has no business riding the rails."

"Whoa!" Fred held up both hands, palms toward Chet. "Will you stop long enough to listen to me?"

Chet crossed his arms over his chest and stared at him.

Fred grinned. "I'm not running away. I came to tell you about the new program FDR came up with. It's called CCC. Have you heard about it?"

Chet shook his head. He had a guarded look in his eyes. "No, I haven't heard about it."

"I wanted to be sure you knew about it before you left the city. That's why I've been looking for you." Fred told him the little bit he knew. By the time he was done, interest sparkled in Chet's eyes.

"Why don't you come home with me?" Fred suggested. "You can learn more about the program."

When they arrived home, all the lights were on in the house. Fred glanced at Chet. "Uh-oh. I think I'm in trouble."

"Didn't they know you were out looking for me?"

"No. I was afraid if I told them, they wouldn't let me go."

"And they shouldn't have," Chet said, "considering where I found you."

"Aw, I was okay." Anger and embarrassment made Fred uncomfortable. *Is that all the thanks I get for going to all that trouble for him?*

He led the way through the back door and into the kitchen.

Mother clasped her hands together. "Thank goodness, you're safe!"

Father was talking on the phone. He glanced at the boys then spoke into the receiver. "It's okay. He just walked in. Sorry to disturb you, officer."

Fred bit back a groan. *Officer! Boy, I'm in more trouble than I thought!*

CHAPTER 17
A Rude Awakening

Father crossed his arms and glared at Fred. "Where have you been?"

"Uh, looking for Chet. I was afraid he'd leave the city before I could tell him about the CCC." *I think I'd rather be back in the jungle than here right now!* Fred thought. His parents didn't get angry with him very often, but when they did, watch out!

Father nodded at Chet. "Glad to see he found you."

Fred breathed a sigh of relief and smiled.

Father's frown grew deeper. "I'm not glad you went out at night without asking permission."

"I'm sorry, sir." Fred dropped his smile. It looked like he wasn't going to get off as easy as he'd hoped.

114

"I was just on the phone to the police when you came in," Father told him.

"Yes, sir."

"I don't ever want to have a reason to call them again, do you understand?"

"Yes, sir."

Fred thought Father's eyes still looked as angry as they had been when he and Chet walked in. "You are going to be grounded for this. I just haven't decided for how long yet."

"Yes, sir. Can you tell Chet more about the CCC now?"

"I'm too angry to talk about it. We'll talk tomorrow, when I've calmed down. Right now, young man, you will head up to bed."

Fred sighed. "Yes, sir." He lifted one hand in a small wave to Chet. "Night."

"Boy, parents can sure get upset over nothing," he muttered, going up the steps to his bedroom. "Why do they have to be so mad? They can see I'm all right. Nothing happened to me. Don't they know I can take care of myself?"

The memory of the long minutes in the jungle came flooding back.

"I guess maybe they did have a good reason to be worried about me." He glanced out the window at the star-filled sky. "And I guess maybe You were looking out for me, God. Thanks."

The next morning after a breakfast of pancakes with depression maple syrup (made with sugar, hot water, and maple flavoring), Father told Chet what he knew about the CCC.

"FDR made this program to get kids like you off the bread lines and the hobo trains," Father told Chet.

Fred tried to watch Chet without staring. It seemed to Fred that Chet's face was filled with eagerness. Chet placed his elbows on the table, leaned forward to listen, and kept his gaze fixed on Father's face.

After Father had told Chet about the camps and the money, he said, "Not everyone who applies will get a job with the CCC. You have to have a physical to show you're healthy enough to do the hard work that will be required. After all, the men and boys in the CCC will be working at hard, physical labor all day long, six days a week."

"I'm not afraid of hard work," Chet told him, "and I'm not a weakling. I'm sure I can pass the physical."

Father smiled. "I think you can, too. Now, one of the other rules is that you have to have dependents."

Chet frowned. "You mean like kids? I'm not even married."

"No, not kids. Just someone who is depending on your money other than you. Like your parents and brothers and sisters."

"That's the best part of this CCC thing." A grin spread across Chet's face. "I can send money home to my family. Twenty-five dollars a month won't make them millionaires, but it will keep food on the table and a roof over their heads. Maybe it will even keep my brothers and sisters in school."

"You'll have to have your parents sign a paper telling the CCC authorities that you are their son, unmarried, and they will be depending on you for the money to support them. Do you think your father will sign such a paper?"

Fred glanced at Chet. Would his father be too embarrassed to sign it? Would he think it was awful to admit he needed his son's help that way?

"I think so, sir," Chet said.

"The enrollment begins in a couple weeks. Maybe we should call your parents. You can tell them about your plans and what they'll need to sign."

Chet's cheeks reddened. "My folks don't have a telephone."

116

"Then I guess you'd better write them."

"Yes, sir. I'll do it today."

Father gave him a stern look. "Another thing. I want you staying here with us from now on. No more of this sleeping in missions and jungles. You need to be as healthy as possible when you apply to the CCC. Besides, I don't want Fred to go looking for you again when the letter comes from your father."

Fred thought Chet looked a bit embarrassed, but he smiled, and his eyes radiated happiness. "Yes, sir."

Father knew the man in charge of the CCC enrollment in the city. He called and asked him what they would need from Chet's father. Then he told Chet what to tell his father in the letter.

For the next week and a half, Chet and Fred watched the mailbox for a letter from Chet's father. Every day, they'd leave the mailbox with a disappointed look on Chet's face.

"My dad can't read and write very well," Chet admitted to Fred one day after they'd checked for the letter that wasn't there. "He never finished school. I'm afraid he won't understand my letter, that he won't know what I need and how soon."

"I'm sure the letter you wrote will explain everything to him real clear," Fred said, trying to reassure his friend. But Fred himself wasn't so sure.

"Maybe they'll be upset because I haven't written them more often," Chet said. "But it's kind of hard to write when you don't know what's happening at home."

"They can't blame you too much for that." Fred spread his hands. "Besides, where would they have sent letters to you? To a hobo jungle?"

Chet shrugged and chuckled. "I guess you're right."

One night, loud whistles woke Fred from a sound sleep. He jerked upright in bed, looking around frantically. In the bed on the other side of the room, Chet was doing the same thing. "What's going on?"

"I don't know," Fred said.

He climbed out of bed and went into the hall. His father and mother and two brothers were coming out of their rooms. Everyone had wide eyes and startled expressions.

"What's going on?" everyone asked.

Then Chet started laughing. "I know what it is. It's April sixth. The whistles are from the beer breweries. They're telling the city it's legal to buy beer again."

Everyone laughed with relief that a big fire hadn't broken out in the city.

As they climbed back into their beds, Fred said, "I wish they'd waited until morning to blow the whistles. They could have got us up for the day instead of in the middle of the night!"

The next day, there still wasn't a letter in the mailbox for Chet.

"If it doesn't come soon, it will be too late," Chet told Fred.

It finally arrived on Saturday.

Chet tore the letter open right away. His eyes shone with joy as he read it. "They say they're glad to hear from me," he told Fred. "They say they've worried about me, whether I was safe and had enough to eat."

Fred just smiled at Chet. *I know his family's love is more important to him than the CCC stuff he needs, but it would embarrass him if I said so.*

Chet grinned at him. "My dad returned the statement your father had me send—the one for the CCC—and he signed it."

Later Chet showed it to Fred's father.

"Good!" Father said. "It's just in time. Enrollment in the CCC begins Monday."

Fred looked at Chet's happy face. Chet *had* to be accepted in the CCC. He just had to!

CHAPTER 18
A New Life for Chet

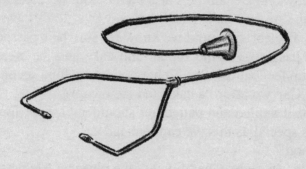

Alice hung the cone-shaped receiver on the side of the wooden wall phone in the kitchen. Excitement was shooting through her. She turned to her mother, who was wiping the supper dishes.

"Guess what! Chet went to apply for the CCC today." Alice's words rushed out.

"Was he accepted?" Mother asked.

"Yes! Well, almost. They told him he's accepted if he passes the physical exam tomorrow at the army recruiting station."

"That's wonderful!"

Alice hurried across the room and leaned against the counter beside her mother. "Do you think we could invite the Allertons and Chet to supper tomorrow night to celebrate? With a cake and ice cream for dessert?"

She held her breath. She'd hardly dared ask! Father's hours and pay weren't very good anymore. The family had become more and more careful about stretching their food dollars. And they already had the Allertons over every other Sunday.

Mother laughed. "Don't you think we should wait until Chet knows for certain he's accepted before we celebrate?"

"But I'm sure he'll pass! Anyway, we don't have to tell him it's a celebration until we know for sure he's passed. If he doesn't pass, maybe the supper and cake and ice cream will make him feel better." She bit her bottom lip for a second, then asked, "Can we afford a cake and ice cream?"

Mother smiled and patted her shoulder. "I think for something as special as this we can manage it."

"Good!"

Alice was right. Chet did pass the physical. He was beaming the next evening at the supper table when he told everyone what came next.

"I'm to report to Fort Snelling," he said.

Fred laughed. "That sounds like you're in the army!"

"That's how they treat us. Army officers will be in charge of the CCC camps. We'll live in camps like soldiers and be given clothes to wear, like uniforms."

Chet tried to make it sound matter-of-fact, but Alice could see he was proud to be treated like a man in the army. "Why do you go there?" she asked.

"It's kind of like an army training camp. We'll be divided into companies, or groups. Then they're going to put us on a program to toughen us up so we can do the work they send us to do."

"I think this sounds like a wonderful program," Alice's mother told Chet. "I'm sure you'll be good at the job."

Chet beamed at her. "A place to sleep, three meals a day, and I'll be paid for it. A man couldn't ask for much more than that."

"It's not just young men like Chet who are going to benefit from this program," Fred's father told everyone, "or their families. There are already reports going out that doctors and nurses will be needed at the camps, and of course, people will need to supply things like food. Things like that will create more jobs. The government's going to pay for everything that's needed."

After a while, they began talking about things other than the CCC.

"Did you know Minnesota's legislature passed a new state income tax?" Alice's father asked. "The money will be used for the schools."

Alice jerked up straight. "Does that mean our schools won't be closed?"

Father grinned. "I think so. But you still want them to close for summer vacation, don't you?"

Alice laughed at her father's joke.

When it was time for dessert, Mother let Alice carry the cake to the dining room. Mother had put it on one of her pretty crystal plates. It was heavy, so Alice carried it carefully and walked slowly. It was so heavy that she almost had to hold her breath when she set it down beside Chet.

"This is for you." She smiled at him. "Congratulations!"

"Thanks, Alice. Did you make this cake?"

She nodded. She had hurried home from school to make it so it would be cool enough to frost before supper.

"That's very nice of you." His smile made all the trouble she'd gone to worthwhile.

Three weeks later, Alice and Dot rode with Fred in the back of his father's car to Fort Snelling. Fred's parents were in front.

"I've kind of missed Chet since he went to Fort Snelling to train," Fred told them. "I was getting used to having him around the house."

Father stuck his arm out the window, straight, to signal a left turn. A minute later, the three children slid into each other as he turned a corner. They straightened up again right away.

"I'm glad he made it into the CCC," Alice said, "but I wish he weren't going to be sent far away from Minneapolis."

Fred nodded. He felt the same way.

Fort Snelling was in St. Paul, across the river from Minneapolis. The fort stood on a bluff overlooking the Mississippi River.

Fred had driven past the fort before, but he'd never been inside it. He liked the old stone walls and round tower. The fort was one of the earliest places non-Indian people lived in Minnesota, other than priests and fur traders. He could easily imagine soldiers and their families in this old fort almost one hundred years ago.

"Soldiers from Minnesota came here when they were sent to the Civil War, the Spanish-American War, and the Great War," Fred told Alice and Dot.

"And now Chet is being sent out with the CCC in the war against unemployment," Father said from the front seat.

Fred hadn't thought of it like that before.

Inside the walls of the fort, they found the young men who were with the CCC. They were all dressed alike, with dark trousers, khaki shirts, and boots. Even their hats and khaki coats were the same. They were all wearing their coats, too. Although it was the first week in May, it was cold.

Fred grinned at Alice. "Dressed alike that way, they do almost look like they're in an army, don't they?"

She nodded. "Yes, they do."

Fred spotted Chet and waved. "Chet! Over here!"

Chet came jogging toward them. After greetings, Fred asked, "Do you know where they're sending you?"

"Yeah. My company is going to the Superior National Forest in northern Minnesota. We'll be cutting trees, thinning them out in overgrown areas, planting trees in others, and even fighting forest fires—if there are any."

They only had time to talk for a couple minutes before there was a call for the company to assemble.

Chet shook hands with Fred's father. Then he shook hands with Fred. Quietly he said, "Thanks, friend. If it weren't for you, I wouldn't be here now."

Then he said a quick good-bye to Fred's mother, Alice, and Dot. "Thanks for coming!" Chet called over his shoulder as he started to jog back toward his company. "I'll write you!"

"You'd better!" Fred called.

An army officer called the company to order. Soon they were marching past wooden barracks toward army transport trucks. They swung their hats above their heads, waving at the family, friends, and newspaper reporters who had come to see them off.

"Every one of them is wearing a grin as wide as the Mississippi," Fred said, grinning himself.

Father nodded. "You can tell how proud every one of them is to be headed to do a man's job. It's hard on a man when, through no fault of his own, he can't support himself."

I wish I were going with them, Fred thought. Of course, he would never be accepted into the CCC, even if he were old enough. He knew that. His father made too much money compared to these young men. Harry had already asked about it, wanting to go himself.

Dot sighed. "I wish there were something like the CCC for married men like my father."

"FDR has been working on that," Fred's father told her.

"Really?" She turned wide, hopeful eyes to him.

It must be awful to always be wondering when your father is going to find a job, Fred thought, watching her.

"Really," Father said. "Congress has passed a law to help unemployed men. It's called NIRA, the National Industrial Relief Act."

Dot shook her head. "I don't care what it's called, just so long as it gives men like Father jobs."

Fred's father laughed. "Is your father going to Washington with the veterans?"

"Not this time. He says he can't afford to be away from his job at the Organized Unemployed for that long. But our family prays every night that President Roosevelt will listen to the veterans and give them their bonuses."

It seemed only a couple minutes before the men were on the transport trucks. Fred waved furiously as the truck carrying Chet passed. Chet waved back with that wide grin still on his face.

A pang of loneliness shot through Fred. He was going to miss Chet a lot. *But I'm glad for him,* he thought. He remembered Chet's words of thanks. *I really am glad for him.*

CHAPTER 19
A Terrible Mistake

The news on the radio and in the newspapers was full of the veterans in Washington the next few days.

"Did you hear that the president met with some of the veterans?" Dot asked when she came to Alice's house one afternoon.

"Yes. And Mrs. Roosevelt met with six hundred disabled veterans on the White House lawn," Alice said. "Nothing like that happened when your father and the other Bonus Marchers were in Washington last year."

"That's for sure."

Later on the news, the reporter told of the president's wife, Eleanor Roosevelt, leading the veterans in Washington through ankle-deep mud, singing "There's a Long, Long Trail A-winding."

Dot and Alice laughed at the picture it created in their minds. They stopped laughing to hear the reporter's next words, for he was still talking about the veterans.

"FDR has announced that twenty-five thousand positions in the CCC will be given to veterans."

Dot gasped. Then she smiled. "I wonder if Father will be one of the men to get a job with the CCC."

Alice hoped so. Her heart hurt for all her friend and her family were going through.

Dot's smile faded. "I don't know if I'd like him to live far away from the family in the north woods, though, like Chet is doing."

Suddenly Dot jumped up and started marching around Alice's living room, singing, "There's a Long, Long Trail A-winding," just as Eleanor Roosevelt had done.

Alice jumped up and followed her, then Steven and Isabel and Frank. Even little Audrey tried to toddle behind them.

Alice's parents laughed as they watched the parade. Then Mother jumped up and followed along, singing at the top of her lungs and clapping her hands in time to the music. Finally they all collapsed in the middle of the living room floor.

"I think Mrs. Roosevelt must be awfully nice," Alice said. "I saw a picture of her in the newspaper one day. She was helping in a soup kitchen."

"She does seem very nice," Mother agreed.

When I grow up, I want to be like Mrs. Roosevelt, Alice thought, *nice and helpful like she is.*

There was an advertisement on the radio for a movie, a comedy with the Marx Brothers. "Oh, that sounds funny, doesn't it?" Alice asked.

"I haven't seen a movie in years," Dot said, with a faraway look in her eyes.

Alice felt uneasy for a minute. Even though she and Dot were good friends, she forgot sometimes how truly poor Dot's family was.

"Oh!" Alice sat up straight. "I just had a marvelous idea!"

"What?" Dot's face was alight with curiosity.

"Let's put on a play. We can invite all the neighbors. No one would have to pay anything."

Alice didn't think Dot looked too excited about her idea.

"Do you know any plays?" Dot asked.

Alice squirmed. "Well, no, but we can think of something. Maybe we can write one."

Dot laughed. "Sure. Like the book we were going to write about the girl detectives in Minneapolis."

"I know! Let's do the Nancy Drew book! All the kids like Nancy Drew stories. At least, all the girls do," Alice amended, "and the boys will if they see the play."

Dot's face lit up again. "That's a great idea."

"Do I get to be in your play?" Mother asked.

Alice shook her head. "Sorry. There isn't a mother in the play."

"But Nancy has a housekeeper," Dot reminded Alice. "Your mother could play her." She looked at Mrs. Harrington. "That is, if you don't mind playing a housekeeper."

Alice's mother smiled. "I don't mind. There's nothing wrong with being a housekeeper. Any work that's necessary and legal is honorable."

Alice thought her mother looked as excited to be in the play as Dot did.

Alice and Dot talked Fred, Steven, and Isabel into being in the play. They also asked some of their friends from school to help. They practiced whenever they could after school and on weekends.

One day Alice handed the Nancy Drew book to Dot. "We've almost worn this book out!"

Dot grinned. "I guess it would be easier if we had more than one copy, but that would cost money."

"Well, I think we're doing okay with one book."

While the children were busy preparing their neighborhood play, FDR and Congress were busy trying to help the country. They passed the Federal Emergency Relief Act, which provided necessities like food for unemployed people and their families. Congress finally passed the Agricultural Adjustment Act, too. "That's the bill to help farmers," Father told Alice. "The one FDR suggested a couple weeks after he became president."

"Why did it take so long for Congress to pass it?" Alice asked. "Farmers need help, don't they?"

"They sure do! Congress didn't like everything FDR wanted in the bill, so the senators and representatives from all forty-eight states had to talk it over for a while before passing it."

"Oh."

The news reporter talked about the farm bill that night. "It's called the Agricultural Adjustment Act, folks, or AAA. Since FDR took office, bills have been flying through Congress. We've had the Emergency Conservation Work Act—that's the ECW; the Civilian Conservation Corps—that's the CCC; the National Industrial Relief Act—that's the NIRA; the Federal Emergency Relief Act—that's the FERA; and the Agricultural Adjustment Act, or AAA. Yes, sir, folks, it looks like FDR's doing real well with his alphabet soup programs."

Alice frowned. "What are the alphabet soup programs?"

"Programs that are known by their initials," Mother

answered. "Every program that passes becomes known by its initials. There are so many programs known by their initials that it's like alphabet soup."

Alice and Steven laughed.

The children were still working hard on their play. Alice's father and mother helped them turn their garage, porch, and backyard into a set for the play. They left one area for the audience.

"At least we don't need costumes," Alice told Dot and Fred. "We can wear our own clothes."

"Except for the guys' hats," Fred reminded her. "I'm borrowing one of Father's hats."

They had even recruited Fred's older brothers, Harry and Larry, to play bad guys in the play. Addy was playing one of the women who had been robbed.

When the children weren't doing their chores or their homework or practicing the play or helping with the set, they were making posters and putting them up around the neighborhood.

The yard was filled with neighbors the night of the play. Dot's mother had made cookies. She sold them for a penny each before the play and during intermission.

The play was a smashing success. "You should charge people to see this," many of the neighbors told them afterward.

Alice was just glad everything went well and everyone enjoyed the play.

The next day was Sunday, and Fred's family was spending it at Alice's home. Alice and Fred looked through the Minneapolis *Tribune* together. At first, Alice didn't pay much attention to the pages in front of them. Her mind was filled with wonderful memories of the play the night before.

"Wow! Look at that!" Fred's voice jolted Alice out of her memories.

She looked at the picture he pointed to. There was a farmer in a cotton field. Alice couldn't really tell what he was doing, so she read the headline beneath the picture. "Cotton farmers destroy their crops to earn AAA money."

"I don't understand," she said. "How can they get paid for destroying their crops?"

"That's not the worst." Anger threaded through Fred's voice. "Read the rest of the article."

Alice read as fast as she could. "Why, farmers are killing their hogs! Six million baby pigs! And they aren't to sell the meat." The very thought of it made her sick to her stomach. "Why would the government pay them to do that? There must be a mistake!"

CHAPTER 20
Blue Eagles

"It's not as bad as it sounds," Father said when Alice and Fred showed him the article.

"But it says the farmers are getting paid for destroying their crops and animals," Fred told him. "Why would they get paid for crops and animals they don't send to market? That doesn't make sense."

"If the farmers try to sell those crops and hogs on the market, the price they are paid will go down. The price for hogs is only two or three cents a pound. It can't go down much farther than that, can it?"

"Why not?" Alice asked.

"Remember when you and Dot made bread?" Father asked.

Alice nodded.

"Remember counting how much money you made selling the bread and comparing it to how much it cost you to make the bread?"

Alice nodded again.

"If it had cost you more to make it than to sell it, what would you have done?"

Alice only had to think about that for a minute. "We would have asked people for more money when we sold the bread, or else we would have just stopped making the bread and selling it."

"Right," Father said. "What if you asked people to pay more money for it, but they wouldn't?"

"I guess we would have sold the bread we'd already made for as much as people would pay. Then we'd stop making bread."

"Why?" Father asked.

Alice shook her head. "That's a silly question. We wouldn't be making any money."

"Exactly right. And that's why farmers are getting rid of their crops and hogs. They can't make any money raising and selling them."

"Chet says that's already happening," Fred said.

Father nodded. "Yes, in many cases, it is. There's already enough cotton in storage from past years that the world doesn't need any cotton at all grown this year."

Fred grinned and wiggled his eyebrows. "This trick of getting money for not raising things sounds pretty easy. Think if I write and tell FDR I'm not raising hogs or cotton, either, that he'll send me some money?"

Alice laughed.

Father chuckled and shook his head.

Fred held out his hands and shrugged. "Well, I thought it was worth a try."

Alice and her mother were walking along the sidewalk, almost to the grocery store. Alice chattered away to her mother about plans to put on the Nancy Drew play for a penny a family at the local YMCA. She didn't bother paying attention to the places they were passing. She'd walked this way many times before.

When they reached the store, Alice started to turn in at the door. Suddenly she noticed Mother wasn't coming to the door. Mother was looking in the windows.

Alice looked in the windows, too. There wasn't anything exciting to see—only some groceries and other household things, which were for sale inside. "What are you looking at?" she asked Mother.

"I'm not looking *at* anything. I'm looking *for* the Blue Eagle."

Alice drew her eyebrows together, puzzled. "What Blue Eagle?"

"The picture of the Blue Eagle that shows the store owner supports FDR's new National Recovery Act, the NRA. It shows the owner supports the president's campaign to get the country back to work."

"I thought everyone wanted more jobs for people," Alice said.

"Everyone does," Mother agreed, "but not everyone agrees with the way the president is trying to go about it. You see, the NRA limits the number of hours an employer can ask an employee to work. It also says employers have to pay at least a certain amount of money to their employees. That's called a minimum wage. The owners of stores with Blue Eagles have signed an agreement saying they will follow that law."

"Oh." To Alice, it all seemed a lot to be thinking about when all they wanted was a few groceries.

"There's another grocery store two blocks from here," Mother said. "Let's see if they have a Blue Eagle."

Alice groaned, but Mother had already started out.

As the days passed, Alice saw Blue Eagles everywhere. Even the grocer who hadn't had one in his window that first day finally put one up.

"Doesn't pay not to sign the agreement and put up the Blue Eagle," Father told her. "Stores that don't have a Blue Eagle lose business."

"Like when Mother and I went to the other grocery store," she said.

"That's right. The mill is even putting Blue Eagles on its flour bags. And Uncle Richard is displaying one at his office."

One evening Dot stopped at Alice's house. She'd been selling bread, but by the time she reached Alice's, she'd sold it all. The only things left in her large basket were the towels she used beneath and over the bread when she carried it from house to house.

Mother picked up the basket Dot had set on the kitchen table and studied it. "What a wonderful basket!"

"Thank you," Dot said. "I made it."

"You *made* it?" Mother asked.

Dot nodded.

Alice stared at her in surprise. "I didn't know you could do that."

"One of my neighbors taught me. It was easy. I made it from twigs and branches. Everyone seems to like it. A lot of the people I sell bread to have said they like it."

"Would you make one for me?" Mother asked. "I'll be glad to pay you for it, of course."

Dot's face brightened. "Sure!"

"Have you sold them to anyone else?" Alice asked.

Dot shook her head. "No."

"I bet if you made some more, other people would buy them," Alice suggested.

"Do you really think so?"

"Yes," Alice said. "They're pretty."

"I think you'll be able to sell them, too," Mother told her.

"Maybe I'll try," Dot said.

Alice grinned at her. "And you told me you didn't know how to make anything you could sell."

Dot grinned back. "Well, I just learned how to make these a couple weeks ago." Alice's statement must have reminded her of Chet's carved birds because she asked, "Has Fred heard anything from Chet since he went to the CCC camp?"

"Only a short thank-you note he wrote to Fred and Uncle Richard. He didn't say much about the camp or what he's doing there, only that he and the other boys are kept very busy."

Dot was at Alice's house the next night during the president's next fireside chat. The girls listened closely. President Roosevelt said that during that year, more than one thousand people a day were losing their homes because they couldn't pay the mortgages.

"People like us," Dot whispered to Alice.

The president said he wanted people to save their homes so he had asked Congress to pass still another law: the Homeowners Loan Act. And they had.

Dot clapped. "Oh, good! The president saved our house!"

"I thought the state governor already said people didn't need to pay their mortgages," Alice said.

"The governor never meant that to be forever," Father told her. "He only meant it to last until the state or federal government passed a law protecting people's houses during these hard times."

"Oh."

Dot looked up at him from the floor, where she and Alice sat. "But with the president's new act, no one will be able to take our house away, will they?"

"That depends," Father said. "The new act might mean your father doesn't have to pay as much money every month for the house, but he will still have to pay something every month. And it will still be a lot of money."

Alice watched as Dot's joy seemed to seep away. She tried to think of something to say to cheer her up. "At least it's better to pay less money each month," she said.

Dot sighed. "Yes, it is."

"Did your father apply for one of the veterans' positions with the CCC, Dot?" Father asked.

"Yes, but he wasn't accepted. He was really hoping he would be, but. . ." Dot's voice trailed off.

Alice hurt for her friend. Mr. Lane worked so hard, but he couldn't get a real job. He was still working with the Organized Unemployed, but he was only paid in scrip, so he had to try making money in other ways, too.

One day, Alice had seen him on a street corner selling apples. It had been near the Foshay Tower, the great building where he'd once worked as a well-paid and admired executive. She knew it must be hard for him to sell apples to people who used to work for him.

I don't understand, God, she prayed that night before she went to bed. *We've been praying for a better job for Mr. Lane for such a long time. Why are You taking so long to answer?*

CHAPTER 21
Surprise Answers

Alice looked about the crowd impatiently. She and her family had been here for at least fifteen minutes. Fred's family and Dot were supposed to meet them here for the Blue Eagle parade. Where were they?

She searched the sea of people. Everywhere she looked, the sidewalk was crowded with women in lightweight summer dresses and men in suits and straw summer hats.

Someone poked her shoulder. She turned around. "Fred! I was beginning to wonder if you were ever going to get here."

His blue eyes sparkled. "We wouldn't miss a parade." He held up an opened envelope. "Look what came today: a letter from Chet!"

"What does he say? Does he like the CCC camp? Have they had much work to do?"

Fred laughed and handed her the envelope. "Here, why don't you read it yourself and find out."

"If you don't think Chet would mind..."

"I'm sure he wouldn't," Fred said. "He says in the letter to say hello to you and Dot."

Alice flashed him a smile. She was in such a hurry to read the letter that she could hardly get it out of the envelope. Quickly she began to read:

Dear Fred,

Well, here I am in the wild north country. They work us hard in the CCC, but as one of my bunkmates says, it sure beats, "Brother, can you spare a dime."

We're staying in tents for now. It's rather like camping out. The leaders tell us we're going to build cabins before winter sets in, though. And he means we are going to build them! That'll be another new experience. Rumor is we're going to use pine logs that were cut many years ago and are at the bottom of a nearby lake. Davy Crockett, move over!

We'll be pretty experienced by the time we build the cabins. There was nothing here when we arrived, so we're making the whole campsite. So far we've built a large mess hall. Right now it's also used for our recreation building, infirmary, and library! We've also built a small garage and a tool-shed. And last but not least, we built and dug a few outhouses! We've yet to start a machine shop and quarters for the army officers who are in charge of our company.

Of course, we do the work we were sent here to do, too. You'd hardly recognize me after the summer I've spent cutting down trees, chopping them up, cleaning up dead trees and brush, removing gooseberry bushes (they cause rust on pine trees), and planting new pines. Why, I have muscles now! Well, no more than any of the other guys, I guess. We were a pretty skinny bunch when we got here. With the hard work and three meals a day, we're beginning to look like regular guys.

A typical day up here goes something like this:

6:00 A.M.: Bugler wakes us up. After making our beds, army style, we dress and head for the mess hall for breakfast.

8:00 A.M.: Each man is assigned to a work group of six to twelve men. Trucks take us as close as the roads go to where we are to work in the forest that day. Then we walk, carrying our axes, saws, and any other tools we need.

1:00 P.M.: The truck driver brings us lunch. Usually something like bologna sandwiches.

4:00 P.M.: Return to camp and clean up.

5:00 P.M.: Supper.

5:30 P.M.: Choice of athletics or use of library—if we aren't working on some building for the camp!

10:30 P.M.: Lights out.

Sundays, a minister comes from a nearby town—well, nearby according to northern Minnesota woods standards!

We already had to help fight one forest fire. Hot work! But it felt good to know we'd done something so important.

After being in the city, it's great living in the woods. There's nothing like the sounds of the woods at night or early in the morning before the bugler rousts the camp.

But best of all is being able to help out my family. They've written me a couple times and say the money I send home is a big help.

Greet all your family for me, Fred, and say hello to Alice and Dot, too. Write me when you get a chance.

Your friend,
Chet

Alice folded the letter and put it back into the envelope. "He sounds pretty happy."

"Yes, I think he is."

"Alice, Fred!"

Alice turned at Dot's voice. She was trying to work her way through the crowd on the sidewalk. Finally she reached them.

"Hi!" Alice said. "Fred got a letter from Chet today. He said to say hello to you. Do you want to read the letter?"

"Later," Dot said. "I have something important to tell you two."

Dot's shining eyes and red cheeks made Alice curious. "What is it?"

140

"What is it, Dot?" Fred repeated.

"Do you remember the president's program?"

Fred and Alice laughed. "Which one?" Fred asked.

"I think it's the one called FERA. Anyway, it's the one where surplus food is given to unemployed people."

Fred and Alice nodded and waited.

"Some of those goods are coming to Minneapolis," Dot told them. "The city needs more people to help decide where to store the goods and who should have them, things like that." She bounced up and down. "They've asked Father to take one of the jobs!"

Alice threw her arms around Dot. "That's wonderful! I knew he'd get a real job one day!"

"It's great news!" Fred said.

"It's a job with lots of responsibility," Dot said when she and Alice stopped hugging. "They needed someone for the job who has experience supervising people and organizing things."

"Your father certainly has that after helping get the Organized Unemployed started," Fred said.

Dot grinned. "That's right. The man who hired Father said he knew he'd be good at the job because of the work he did for Organized Unemployed."

"At least at this job, he'll get paid real money," Fred said.

Dot nodded. "Of course, he won't be making nearly as much money as he made when he worked at the Foshay Tower, but he says we'll be able to pay the mortgage each month now! No one will be able to take our house away!"

Alice squeezed her hands. "I'm so glad for you."

Dot smiled. "You know, I didn't want to say anything, but I've been mad at God for giving Father that job at Organized Unemployed that only paid in scrip—and not much of that. But all along, God was using that job to get Father this good job!"

Band music stirred the air. The crowd started looking down the street, standing on tiptoes and looking around the people in front of them. "The parade is starting!"

The band, dressed in smart, colorful uniforms, marched by playing "Happy Days Are Here Again!" Alice, Dot, and Fred joined the rest of the crowd singing the cheerful words. People about them waved small flags with Blue Eagles on them.

After the band came people carrying banners with the names of companies who had signed the pledge to become Blue Eagle companies. As far as Alice could see down the street, there were more people and more banners.

Happiness swelled up within her. There were still a lot of people without jobs, but things were getting better. *Maybe what Mother said is true,* Alice thought, watching the banners with Blue Eagles pass by. *Maybe learning to love and help each other* is *the most important thing God is teaching us.*

There's More!

The American Adventure continues with *Starting Over*. Alice's father has lost his job, and there's no way the large Harrington family can continue to live in Minneapolis. So all nine Harringtons sell most of their possessions, load up their car, and head west.

Will their old car travel two thousand miles without breaking down? Will they have enough money to make it to Seattle? And once they arrive, will Father find work? Mother thinks it's a great adventure in faith, but Frank and Isabel aren't so sure.

You're in for the ultimate

American Adventure!

Collect all 48 books!

The Plymouth Period (1620-1634)

1) *The Mayflower Adventure*
   ISBN 1-57748-059-7
2) *Plymouth Pioneers*
   ISBN 1-57748-060-0
3) *Dream Seekers* ISBN 1-57748-073-2

The Boston Period (1635-1808)

4) *Fire by Night* ISBN 1-57748-074-0
5) *Queen Anne's War*
   ISBN 1-57748-146-1
6) *Danger in the Harbor*
   ISBN 1-57748-147-X
7) *Smallpox Strikes!* ISBN 1-57748-144-5
8) *Maggie's Choice* ISBN 1-57748-145-3
9) *Boston Revolts!* ISBN 1-57748-156-9
10) *The Boston Massacre*
    ISBN 1-57748-157-7
11) *The American Revolution*
    ISBN 1-57748-158-5
12) *The American Victory*
    ISBN 1-57748-159-3
13) *Adventure in the Wilderness*
    ISBN 1-57748-230-1

The Cincinnati Period (1808-1865)

14) *Earthquake in Cincinnati*
    ISBN 1-57748-231-X
15) *Trouble on the Ohio River*
    ISBN 1-57748-232-8
16) *Escape from Slavery*
    ISBN 1-57748-233-6
17) *Cincinnati Epidemic*
    ISBN 1-57748-255-7
18) *Riot in the Night* ISBN 1-57748-256-5
19) *Fight for Freedom*
    ISBN 1-57748-257-3
20) *Enemy or Friend?*
    ISBN 1-57748-258-1
21) *Danger on the Railroad*
    ISBN 1-57748-259-X
22) *Time for Battle* ISBN 1-57748-260-3
23) *The Rebel Spy* ISBN 1-57748-267-0
24) *War's End* ISBN 1-57748-268-9

The Minneapolis Period (1876-1935)

25) *Centennial Celebration*
    ISBN 1-57748-287-5
26) *The Great Mill Explosion*
    ISBN 1-57748-288-3
27) *Lights for Minneapolis*
    ISBN 1-57748-289-1
28) *The Streetcar Riots*
    ISBN 1-57748-290-5
29) *Chicago World's Fair*
    ISBN 1-57748-291-3
30) *A Better Bicycle* ISBN 1-57748-292-1
31) *The New Citizen*
    ISBN 1-57748-392-8
32) *The San Francisco Earthquake*
    ISBN 1-57748-393-6
33) *Marching with Sousa*
    ISBN 1-57748-406-1
34) *Clash with the Newsboys*
    ISBN 1-57748-407-X
35) *Prelude to War*
    ISBN 1-57748-410-X
36) *The Great War* ISBN 1-57748-411-8
37) *The Flu Epidemic*
    ISBN 1-57748-451-7
38) *Women Win the Vote*
    ISBN 1-57748-452-5
39) *Battling the Klan*
    ISBN 1-57748-453-3
40) *The Bootlegger Menace*
    ISBN 1-57748-454-1
41) *Black Tuesday* ISBN 1-57748-474-6
42) *The Great Depression*
    ISBN 1-57748-475-4

The Seattle Period (1935-1945)

43) *Starting Over* ISBN 1-57748-509-2
44) *Changing Times* ISBN 1-57748-510-6
45) *Rumblings of War*
    ISBN 1-57748-511-4
46) *War Strikes* ISBN 1-57748-512-2
47) *The Home Front* ISBN 1-57748-513-0
48) *Coming Home* ISBN 1-57748-514-9